**New Directions for
Teaching and Learning**

Catherine M. Wehlburg
EDITOR-IN-CHIEF

Landmark Issues in Teaching and Learning:
A Look Back at New Directions for Teaching and Learning

Marilla D. Svinicki
Catherine M. Wehlburg
EDITORS

Number 123 • Fall 2010
Jossey-Bass
San Francisco

LANDMARK ISSUES IN TEACHING AND LEARNING: A LOOK BACK AT NEW
DIRECTIONS FOR TEACHING AND LEARNING
Marilla D. Svinicki, Catherine M. Wehlburg (eds.)
New Directions for Teaching and Learning, no. 123
Catherine M. Wehlburg, Editor-in-Chief

Microfilm copies of issues and articles are available in 16mm and 35mm,
as well as microfiche in 105mm, through University Microfilms, Inc.,
300 North Zeeb Road, Ann Arbor, MI 48106-1346.

NEW DIRECTIONS FOR TEACHING AND LEARNING (ISSN 0271-0633, elec-
tronic ISSN 1536-0768) is part of The Jossey-Bass Higher and Adult
Education Series and is published quarterly by Wiley Subscription
Services, Inc., A Wiley Company, at Jossey-Bass, 989 Market Street, San
Francisco, CA 94103-1741. Periodicals postage paid at San Francisco,
CA, and at additional mailing offices. POSTMASTER: Send address
changes to New Directions for Teaching and Learning, Jossey-Bass, 989
Market Street, San Francisco, CA 94103-1741.

New Directions for Teaching and Learning is indexed in CIJE: Current
Index to Journals in Education (ERIC), Contents Pages in Education
(T&F), Current Abstracts (EBSCO), Educational Research Abstracts
Online (T&F), ERIC Database (Education Resources Information
Center), Higher Education Abstracts (Claremont Graduate University),
and SCOPUS (Elsevier).

SUBSCRIPTIONS cost $89 for individuals and $259 for institutions, agencies,
and libraries in the United States. Prices subject to change.

EDITORIAL CORRESPONDENCE should be sent to the editor-in-chief,
Catherine M. Wehlburg, c.wehlburg@tcu.edu.

www.josseybass.com

CONTENTS

FROM THE SERIES EDITOR

About This Publication

Since 1980, *New Directions for Teaching and Learning (NDTL)* has brought a unique blend of theory, research, and practice to leaders in postsecondary education. *NDTL* sourcebooks strive not only for solid substance but also for timeliness, compactness, and accessibility.

The series has four goals: to inform readers about current and future directions in teaching and learning in postsecondary education, to illuminate the context that shapes these new directions, to illustrate these new directions through examples from real settings, and to propose ways in which these new directions can be incorporated into still other settings.

This publication reflects the view that teaching deserves respect as a high form of scholarship. We believe that significant scholarship is conducted not only by researchers who report results of empirical investigations, but also by practitioners who share disciplinary reflections about teaching. Contributors to *NDTL* approach questions of teaching and learning as seriously as they approach substantive questions in their own disciplines, and they deal not only with pedagogical issues but also with the intellectual and social context in which these issues arise. Authors deal on the one hand with theory and research and on the other with practice, and they translate from research and theory to practice and back again.

About This Volume

Dr. Marilla Svinicki has been the editor-in-chief of *New Directions for Teaching and Learning* since the early 1990s. As of January, 2010, Dr. Catherine Wehlburg has taken this position. To mark the transition, this issue focuses on the progress of teaching and learning in higher education with regard to some important topics that have shaped it during the life of *New Directions for Teaching and Learning*. This jointly-edited issue is based on a series of landmark developments in the last 30 years. The chapter authors were chosen because of their leadership in the field for their particular topic and each has provided a critical perspective that has made a difference in higher education during the last three decades. We hope that this issue will provide an overview of where these important topics came from, where it is presently, and where it is likely to go in the future. This volume provides the opportunity to trace the evolution of some of today's most important development in teaching and learning.

Catherine M. Wehlburg
Editor-in-Chief

CATHERINE M. WEHLBURG is the assistant provost for Institutional Effectiveness at Texas Christian University.

Preface

Times of transition are often marked by parties or public events. Consider this issue of *New Directions for Teaching and Learning (NDTL)* as your invitation to our ongoing party. We are celebrating the transition from one editor-in-chief to another, and we are using this opportunity to reflect on the impact that this resource has had on higher education. Several landmark issues have been identified that are explored within this volume.

In the first chapter, the outgoing editor-in-chief, Marilla Svinicki, gives an overview of *NDTL* and how it has been a part of the higher education experience since 1980. The second chapter, by Karl Smith, explores how the social basis for learning has been approached through *NDTL* and in higher education. Sally Kuhlenschmidt and Barbara Kacer consider how technology was used in classrooms fifty years ago compared to what one might find in 2010 in the third chapter. In the fourth chapter, Edward Zlotkowski and Donna Duffy discuss the history of community-based learning and the development of service learning as it impacts higher education. The fifth chapter, by Catherine Wehlburg, discusses many of the historical reasons why we view assessment and the evaluation of teaching in the ways that we do. John Tagg, in the sixth chapter, focuses on the learning-paradigm campus and how meaningful feedback can impact institutions as well as individuals. In the seventh chapter, Pat Hutchings brings her perspective on the scholarship of teaching and learning and how this has changed over the past twenty-five years. The eighth chapter, by Marilla Svinicki, focusing on self-regulated learning, has important historical dimensions that contribute to how it can be used to impact student learning. In the ninth chapter, Mike Theall describes how a careful evaluation of teaching can benefit teachers, students, and the entire institution. Finally, Catherine Wehlburg, the incoming editor-in-chief, explores some of the possible trends in the future of higher education and the role *NDTL* may play.

Marilla D. Svinicki
Catherine M. Wehlburg
Editors

MARILLA D. SVINICKI is a professor of educational psychology at the University of Texas at Austin and former director of the Center for Teaching Effectiveness at the same institution. She has been active in faculty development since 1973 and served for two terms as the executive director of the POD Network.

CATHERINE M. WEHLBURG is the assistant provost for Institutional Effectiveness at Texas Christian University. She has taught psychology and educational psychology courses for more than a decade, serving as department chair for some of that time, and then branched into faculty development and assessment. Dr. Wehlburg has worked with both the Higher Learning Commission of the North Central Association and the Commission on Colleges with the Southern Association of Colleges and Schools as an outside evaluator.

1

New Directions for Teaching and Learning was first published in 1980. Since that time, there have been some changes, but many aspects have remained. NDTL issues are designed for faculty across the disciplines and are written in a way that they can be read easily and widely. This provides an important and distinctive variety of perspectives.

The Role of New Directions for Teaching and Learning in Documenting Changes in Postsecondary Education

Marilla D. Svinicki

In 1980 this quarterly sourcebook series, *New Directions for Teaching and Learning*, began its long run under the guidance of one of the leading educators of the time, Kenneth Eble. It is notable that Eble was not a professor of education or psychology or any of the other social sciences identified with teaching, but rather a professor of English. That fact highlights the tenor of the times—that there were not many who actually studied teaching at the postsecondary level as a discipline. What was available to inform teachers were the insights of other teachers into their practice. In addition there were not that many publications that focused on teaching in higher education, especially at the level comprehensible and usable by the typical faculty member. In fact, although there has been an increase in the number of journals that publish content of interest to postsecondary education faculty, such as *Change, College Teaching, Innovative Higher Education*, and *Journal of Excellence in College Teaching*, *New Directions for Teaching and Learning* (NDTL) occupies a distinctive niche among them. Although some journals publish editorials or descriptive articles on matters that affect teaching in higher education and others are starting to publish research into teaching at that level, *NDTL* combines the best of both worlds by putting the practical descriptions, underlying theories, evidence-based research, and examples of new teaching issues across institutions or disciplines. The initial issue set the tone for the rest of the series by focusing on teaching styles of faculty and how they develop and can be modified. The chapters ranged from an attempt to define teaching style and speculate on its origins as a concept to discussions of different styles that were prevalent at the time. Faculty development was just getting started, so several chapters dealt with how one helped an instructor understand and modify his or her style, a topic that has continued to be presented and refined in subsequent issues as more and more was learned about why faculty teach the way they do.

Over the years, the series has continued to have editors who can look at the field both from 30,000 feet and from ground level, starting with Eble and including John Noonan, Robert Young, Robert Menges, and finally me, Marilla Svinicki. In fact, when Menges was asked to take over the editorial responsibilities, he specifically tapped me to work with him because we represented those two levels of understanding. He was a theorist and philosopher of higher education who understood the big picture, and I was a faculty developer working directly with faculty and students in real settings. That combination gave us a good breadth of knowledge as well as the experience with which to anticipate the needs of the field.

During its existence, *NDTL* drew heavily on faculty development and education for its content and issue editors, always with the idea that faculty from across the disciplines should be able to read and apply the ideas highlighted in each issue to their own situation with a minimum of jargon or complex explanations. Although authors have occasionally chafed at the requirement to appeal to a wide audience, most find that writing for *NDTL* brings their work to a whole new constituency, one that is in a position to make the kinds of changes that the authors are championing. As a result the series has been able to involve authors from across the disciplines both to provide theoretical and research-based information about a new finding and to show how the theory can be put into practice in college classrooms and other higher education settings.

Characteristics of *New Directions*

In addition to its focus on postsecondary education, *NDTL* has had several other distinct qualities that have endeared it to the practitioners in the field. As the name implies, it tries to focus on what is new in the field. So as new teaching strategies began to surface, *NDTL* tried to catch them at a stage where their procedures and results were stable enough to provide someone with a good enough picture to evaluate whether or not that strategy would fit their particular circumstances, but not so stable that they were "old hat." In addition, where research data on effectiveness were available, they were included. This latter has especially been assisted by the rise of the Scholarship of Teaching and Learning movement. We can now point to ways in which faculty have been able to validate their strategies and study them in the classroom.

NEW DIRECTIONS FOR TEACHING AND LEARNING • DOI: 10.1002/tl

An important complement to the newness of the topics is *NDTL*'s ability to turn manuscripts around in a very short period of time. As opposed to some trade books that take two years minimum from idea to published work, *NDTL* takes approximately six months from the time of a completed draft to its release to the public. Many issue editors come to us with a plan all mapped out and contributing authors identified, so that the time from idea to submission is also very short. In addition, most authors were either experts in the topic of their chapter or the actual faculty who implemented the new strategy. In both cases, therefore, the chapter authors generally were close to the topic and could write with immediacy. This allowed *NDTL* to bring new ideas to the field quickly while they were still new.

As was mentioned earlier, *NDTL* issues were meant for faculty across the disciplines. This meant that the writing needed to be straightforward and concise so that faculty could read and comprehend the content quickly. Part of this characteristic results from the fact that authors from different disciplines are often chosen to bring the perspective of their own field to an analysis of a new strategy. This variety of perspectives not only allows a reader to find a context that more closely matches his or her own, but also allows the editor to insist that the authors write for an audience of nonspecialists. This cuts down on discipline-specific vocabulary and the assumption that the reader is already well versed in the content in which the new methods are being taught. Like students, the readers will be coming to the text as good learners, but unschooled in the discipline's idiosyncrasies. Such an audience forces the writers to be friendlier to the readers. We take pride in the fact that *NDTL* is read and used by faculty in a wide range of subject areas.

Because *NDTL* came somewhat out of the faculty development movement of the 1970s, its chapters are designed for modularization rather than to be read as a continuous stream. As faculty development was growing in importance, there came a need for printed material to support faculty learning about teaching and learning. Most trade books are written to be read as a whole, but faculty are generally more interested in short but complete articles that do not take too much time out of their busy lives. Faculty developers were grateful to have a single chapter outlining a new method and illustrating it with real class examples, so they found *NDTL* to be a perfect source. In addition, even the entire issues tended to be relatively short and compact. Their low price per issue also gave a good incentive to provide them to faculty at workshops or conferences. Not only would the faculty feel rewarded for participating, but they might even take the opportunity to read in greater depth about a topic. As anyone who is in faculty development knows, most programs run on a small, tight budget, so providing *NDTL* issues allowed faculty to be rewarded without breaking the programs. Conference organizers also recognized this quality of *NDTL*, and several issues were written specifically with an upcoming conference in mind. Copies were often included as one of the benefits of attending the conference. An example of such an issue was No. 116 in 2008 by Michaelsen, Sweet, and Parmelee on team-based learning. Its publication coincided with a national conference on team-based learning, and those in attendance received a copy of the issue.

Another format for issue topics in recent years has been the report of a single campus project focusing on their implementation of a new curriculum idea or a new faculty development project. For example, issue No. 98 by Pace and Middendorf reported on a campus-wide project they referred to as "decoding the disciplines." In this project, faculty from across the campus worked together to understand how students think and learn in their fields, using a methodology that the authors had developed along with the participating faculty. The value of such a format is that faculty from a wide range of disciplines can see a particular strategy implemented in several disciplines and take away from that those things that they have in common while acknowledging their differences.

Some issues dealt with a single general topic, but dealt with it in depth. For example, issue No. 78 by Theall brought an array of perspectives on motivation written by experts in psychology to the faculty in general. This very important topic is one that most faculty recognize as an area in which they have a lot to learn, but no easy, recognized, central source for learning it. Most other books on motivation either focus on the K–12 system or are more in the line of self-help books. *New Directions for Teaching and Learning* brought the experts together and asked them to translate the area for their faculty colleagues. A similar translation of the field of learning science was made in issue No. 89 by Halpern and Hakel (2002) when they turned a report from the American Psychological Association into a set of chapters outlining what was known about learning as revealed by research in psychology.

One final characteristic of *NDTL* that is less obvious to the eye is that it serves as one of the few repositories of fugitive literature in higher education. As Lee Shulman reminds us, those of us in postsecondary education are not in the habit of making our findings public through publishing or even presenting them at conferences. This failure on our part led to a constant reinventing of the wheel of teaching and learning, because there were so few places where such information was made available. I have often found that when writing about postsecondary education, *NDTL* is one of my best sources to find the beginning and progress of new ideas in teaching. Perhaps it would be better to say that *NDTL* is one of the sources that actually shows up in bibliographic searches, making information about teaching much more accessible and more likely that a novice will find it. As Google Scholar and other information-searching supports become a staple of our scholarly work, it is possible that the kinds of ideas currently presented in *NDTL* will start showing up more easily, but for a long time, *NDTL* was one of the few places to find a compilation of information about a given trend.

NEW DIRECTIONS FOR TEACHING AND LEARNING • DOI: 10.1002/tl

Topics That Recur Regularly

Although *NDTL* is mostly targeting new ideas on teaching and learning, we also recognize that as the field grows, so does our understanding of even the most consistent of topics. So in addition to issues that showcase new strategies for teaching and learning, there have been many topics that have been repeated and updated. It is possible that these represent a core curriculum of teaching and learning at the college level.

Research on Learning. Obviously one topic that is both constant and changing is what we need to know about learning. As a core area of knowledge for faculty and also a research area for a great many in psychology, the area of learning has been a frequent topic in *NDTL* and will continue to recur in the future. Some issues dealt directly with research on learning, such as the one by Halpern and Hakel mentioned earlier. The recent incarnation of research on learning shows up in *NDTL* issues that focus on the Scholarship of Teaching and Learning (SOTL). Some early issues that preceded SOTL were those that dealt with classroom research and classroom assessment (issue Nos. 46 and 75), edited by Tom Angelo.

Another related topic to research on learning is understanding student development. How students change across their years in college and how faculty can take those changes into account has been discussed by Marcia Baxter-Magolda in issue No. 82 in terms of intellectual and emotional development and in issue No. 63 by Paul Pintrich in terms of their growth as self-regulating learners.

Strategies for Teaching. Perhaps the bulk of the issues of *NDTL* were designed to introduce new ideas in teaching. For example, issues have focused on problem-based learning, service-learning, technology (of many types) and learning, writing as a teaching strategy, learning communities (of both students and faculty), active learning, teaching with groups, and many more. These issues usually contain many examples of implementation in a variety of settings, along with the reaction of the faculty and students involved.

Evaluation of Teaching. It is not surprising that this is a recurring topic when you remember just how important this topic is to faculty, students, and administrators. Issues on this topic sometimes are intended to defend the use of student evaluations by providing a review of the research into their qualities. Other issues focus on using evaluations to improve teaching. More recent issues have described new ways to evaluate teaching through the use of technology, such as issue No. 96 by Sorenson and Johnson (2003). There is no doubt that this topic will continue to be reviewed regularly in future issues as new ideas are tried and succeed or fail.

Implications of Diversity in Students and Faculty. The decades through which *NDTL* has been published coincide with the expanding recognition of the importance of a diverse student and faculty population.

New Directions for Teaching and Learning has addressed both topics across the years from issue No.16 in 1983 edited by Cones, Noonan, and Janha, through issue No. 111 in 2007 by Kaplan and Miller.

Technology in Teaching and Learning. It would be hard to think of a more game-changing development in teaching and learning than the growth and increasing sophistication of technology support for both activities. The earliest issue on this topic was in 1982, when Christopher Knapper served as editor for issue No. 9. The most recent issue dealing with this topic is No. 114 by Margit Watts on information literacy. *New Directions for Teaching and Learning* has seen the sophistication of both the technology and its users expand with no end in sight, although there does seem to be a shift in the focus of technology away from the hardware and toward empowering the learner to use the technology.

Faculty Development Issues. Given that *NDTL* and faculty development grew up together, it is no surprise that many of the issues have dealt with faculty development. Sometimes it was the practice of faculty development itself, which was the topic of the very first issue in 1980 by Eble to issue No. 79 in 1999 on using consultants to improve teaching by Knapper and Piccinin. Other issues focused on faculty and how they change across their careers—from an early issue (No. 19) by Mehrotra (1984) on faculty and aging to issues that punctuate a faculty member's career, starting as a teaching assistant (No. 39, Nyquist, Abbott, and Wulff, 1989), becoming a junior faculty member (No. 50, Sorcinelli and Austin, 1992), through senior faculty positions (No. 55, Finkelstein and LaCelle-Peterson, 1993). The most recent issue, edited by Hendrix and Hamlet (No. 120, 2009) deals with spirituality in faculty life. These issues are truly a wide net to capture the life and times of the faculty member.

Trends Across the Life of *NDTL*

If you were to think about the changes that have happened in postsecondary education since 1980, you would see that *NDTL* has been reflecting many of them in its issues. We have witnessed a movement from teaching to learning as described in the Barr and Tagg (1995) article on the learning paradigm. Psychology has given us many insights into how students learn (or don't) and why they do what they do (or don't), making it easier for teachers to tap into existing learning and motivation strategies in order to improve learning. This increasing awareness of the role that students play in their own learning is reflected in the articles in this issue of *NDTL*, including those by Smith on group learning and by Svinicki on student self-regulation.

Accompanying the increased emphasis on student-centered teaching and learning is the movement toward recognizing the scholarship of teaching, as proposed by Boyer in 1999. Along with other professions, faculty in postsecondary settings are being encouraged to reflect on their actions as professionals so that they can continue to respond to the changing environment. This increased interpretation of teaching as a worthy scholarly activity is reflected in the articles in this issue by Tagg on the learning campus, and Hutchings on the growth of the scholarship of teaching and learning. The role that evaluation can play in supporting this personal growth is supported by increasing understanding of how we can evaluate teaching, as discussed in the article by Theall and the one by Wehlburg.

Finally we recognize that the classroom is no longer the only venue for learning. The growth of technology to take the classroom to the students and the increase in service learning to take the students to a different classroom are highlighted within this issue in the articles by Kuhlenschmidt and Kacer and by Zlotkowski and Duffy, respectively.

Each of these developments has been spotlighted by issues of *NDTL* across its thirty-year history. What the future holds we cannot accurately predict, but the change of editors for the series opens up even more possibilities and perspectives so that the series as a whole can continue to serve as an important touchstone for changes and trends in higher education.

MARILLA D. SVINICKI is a professor of educational psychology at the University of Texas at Austin and former director of the Center for Teaching Effectiveness at the same institution. She has been active in faculty development since 1973 and served for two terms as the executive director of the POD Network.

NEW DIRECTIONS FOR TEACHING AND LEARNING • DOI: 10.1002/tl

2

The social basis of learning is a concept that has been embraced by the higher educating community. Since the 1980s, there has been exciting growth and the development of specific practices that better engage students in academic content.

Social Basis of Learning: From Small-Group Learning to Learning Communities

Karl A. Smith

It is indeed an honor to be invited to contribute to the thirtieth-anniversary volume of *New Directions for Teaching and Learning*. I recall my delight when I discovered the series, because it contained practical advice that was grounded in theory and promising practices. In 1980 I was an early-career engineering faculty member who was deeply interested in student learning. I was beginning to implement cooperative learning in my classes and was looking for ideas and resources, and especially for a community of like-minded colleagues.

My first encounter with the social basis of learning occurred in about 1974 in a Social Psychology of Education course taught by one of David Johnson's Ph.D. students, Dennis Falk (currently a Professor of Social Work at the University of Minnesota-Duluth). I began taking courses in the College of Education in the early 1970s because I had an overwhelming sense that there was a better way to help engineering students learn than what I was doing, which was essentially what had been done to me; that is, lectures, homework assignments, and individual exams. This overwhelming sense of a better way of doing things was prompted by questions the students asked, which revealed that they had no idea what I was talking about. A representative setting was a course in thermodynamics and kinetics—very abstract areas involving a lot of mathematics—where I was "teaching as taught." My sense that there was a better way was grounded in

NEW DIRECTIONS FOR TEACHING AND LEARNING, no. 123, Fall 2010 © Wiley Periodicals, Inc.
View this article online at wileyonlinelibrary.com. • DOI: 10.1002/tl.405

my training and experience as an engineer, where one of the fundamental ideas was "advancing the state of the art." What I encountered in the Social Psychology of Education course, however, changed my life.

During the first session, Professor Falk assigned us to groups, which was a bit of a surprise to me, as I don't think I had ever experienced this before. He said that there was a lot of dense content and many difficult concepts in the course, and that some of us could probably manage by ourselves but most would benefit from interacting with others. He stressed the ideas of interdependence and accountability, and modeled them through a series of group exercises and assignments. The emphasis on interdependence and accountability was a revelation for me, because it was familiar. This was the way I worked as an engineer on the job and in my research setting. Interdependence and accountability were central to success! At that moment I thought, "Why don't we do this in engineering classes?" The rest, some will say, is history, as cooperative learning is now embraced by many engineering faculty, and its use is increasing by faculty at large, as indicated by the UCLA Higher Education Research Institute Survey of Faculty, as shown in Table 2.1 (DeAngelo and others, 2009).

My intention in this review of the social basis of learning is to summarize contributions on this topic to the *New Directions for Teaching and Learning* (abbreviated *NDTL*) series and connect them to events occurring more broadly.

Table 2.1. The American College Teacher: National Norms for 2007–2008

Methods Used in "All" or "Most" Classes	All Faculty 2005 (%)	All Faculty 2008 (%)	Assistant 2008 (%)
Cooperative learning	48	59	66
Group projects	33	36	61
Grading on a curve	19	17	14
Term/research papers	35	44	47

Social Basis of Learning in Inaugural Issues of *New Directions for Teaching and Learning*

Kenneth Eble, editor of *NDTL* 1 (1980), titled "*Improving Teaching Styles*," writes, "Every teacher develops a particular way of going about the complex task of teaching, and those distinctive characteristics of behavior and approach make up what is identified as teaching 'style'." (Eble, 1980, p. vii). The social nature of learning is included in this inaugural issue, most prominently in Edward Glassman's article. Glassman (1980) features

NEW DIRECTIONS FOR TEACHING AND LEARNING • DOI: 10.1002/tl

cooperative learning, and elaborates on his 1978 article in *Biochemical Education*, "Teaching Biochemistry in Cooperative Learning Groups."

Joseph Axelrod also has an intriguing article in the first volume (Axelrod, 1980). He refers to his 1973 book *The University Teacher as Artist* (Axelrod, 1973), in which he articulates several "teacher mental images about teaching," as shown in Table 2.2.

Axelrod's taxonomy provides a fascinating perspective on the era, and a window into the future. Prior to the Barr and Tagg (1995) and Campbell and Smith (1997) arguments on the shift from teacher-centered to student-centered learning, most of the emphasis was on the teacher and "teacher styles." One of the first places the comparison of old and new paradigms of teaching appeared was Johnson, Johnson, and Smith (1991). See Table 2.3.

Table 2.2. Teacher Mental Images About Teaching (Axelrod, 1973)

Mental Image	Motto	Characteristics	Disciplines
Content	I teach what I know	Pour it in, lecture	Science, math
Instructor	I teach what I am	Modeling, demonstration	Many
Student—cognitive development	I train minds	Active learning, discussion	English, humanities
Student—development of whole person	I work with students as people	Motivation, self-esteem	Basic skills teachers

Table 2.3. Comparison of Old and New Paradigm of Teaching

	Old Paradigm	New Paradigm
Knowledge	Transferred from faculty to students	Jointly constructed by students and faculty
Students	Passive vessel to be filled by faculty's knowledge	Active constructor, discoverer, transformer of knowledge
Faculty purpose	Classify and sort students	Develop students' competencies and talents
Relationships	Impersonal relationships among students and between faculty and students	Personal transaction among students and between faculty and students
Context	Competitive/individualistic	Cooperative learning in classroom and cooperative teams among faculty
Teaching assumption	Any expert can teach	Teaching is complex and requires considerable training

The comparison of old and new paradigms was updated by Smith and Waller (1997), and the figure has been cited many times, and reproduced in numerous publications, such as Colander (2004).The second issue, *Learning, Cognition, and College Teaching*, edited by Wilbert McKeachie, continues to set the stage for powerful connections between research and practice. Distributed throughout the second issue are important features of the social nature of learning, such as McKeachie's (1980) citation of research on surface versus deep processing and the importance of instructor strategies to facilitate deep processing.

Research on "deep learning" is still very active, and a recent article explores connections between student engagement and deep learning, especially in terms of disciplinary differences (NelsonLaird and others, 2008).

Social Basis of Learning Throughout the Thirty Years of *New Directions for Teaching and Learning*

Over the thirty-year history of *New Directions for Teaching and Learning*, the social nature of learning was emphasized in at least 15 issues (out of 120 or 12.5%), numbers 1, 2, 14, 32, 41, 42, 47, 59, 67, 74, 81, 95, 108, 116, and 117; and it was the central feature of many of these.

New Directions for Teaching and Learning No. 14, *Learning in Groups*, edited by Clark Bouton and Russell Garth (1983), was transformative for me, and raised the prominence of the social basis of learning. The entire issue was devoted to the theory and practice of small-group learning, and I found this level of emphasis very reassuring. Influential chapters for me included "Teachers and Learning Groups: Dissolution of the Atlas Complex" (Finkel and Monk, 1983) and "Developing Student Skills and Abilities" (Bouton and Rice, 1983).

The National Institute of Education (1984) report, *Involvement in Learning: Revitalizing Involvement in Learning: Realizing the Potential of American Higher Education. Final Report of the Study Group on the Conditions of Excellence in American Higher Education*, was published in 1984, as was Astin's (1984) "Student Involvement" article. The congruence of support for the social basis of learning provided by this work on the importance of student involvement in learning strengthened my resolve to focus in this area, and I think helped build the foundation of support that influenced the broader community.

A couple of the *NDTL* volumes, 32 and 81, focused on large classes, and included several chapters emphasizing the social basis of learning. Examples include Frederick's (1987) article "Student Involvement: Active Learning in Large Classes," and the Cooper and Robinson (2000) article "The Argument for Making Large Classes Seem Small." Teaching large classes well is an ongoing challenge for college and university faculty, and many books and articles have been written to help faculty, such as Stanley and Porter (2002).

NEW DIRECTIONS FOR TEACHING AND LEARNING • DOI: 10.1002/tl

The late 1980s and early 1990s was a landmark period for supporting and advancing the social basis of learning. In 1987 the "Seven Principles for Good Practice in Undergraduate Education" was published in the *AAHE Bulletin* (Chickering and Gamson, 1987). Three of the seven principles emphasized the social basis of learning: Good practice encourages student-faculty contact, good practice encourages cooperation among students, and good practice encourages active learning. Chickering and Gamson followed up on the *AAHE Bulletin* article in volume 47 (1991), *Applying the Seven Principles for Good Practice in Undergraduate Education*. Gamson (1991) noted in her history of the Seven Principles that more than 150,000 copies were ordered directly from the Johnson Foundation and, since it wasn't copyrighted, an unknown (and likely very large) number of copies were distributed electronically. The publication of the "Seven Principles for Good Practice in Undergraduate Education" was a marker event and provided enormous support for the change from competitive and individualistic learning to cooperative learning.

Several research studies supporting the social basis of learning were published during this period. Pascarella and Terenzini (1991) discussed the importance of engaging students in their synthesis of research about how college affects students, "Perhaps the strongest conclusion that can be made is the least surprising. Simply put, the greater the student's involvement or engagement in academic work or in the academic experience of college, the greater his or her level of knowledge acquisition and general cognitive development . . . If the level of involvement were totally determined by individual student motivation, interest, and ability, the above conclusion would be uninteresting as well as unsurprising. However, a substantial amount of evidence indicates that there are instructional and programmatic interventions that not only increase a student's active engagement in learning and academic work but also enhance knowledge acquisition and some dimensions of both cognitive and psychosocial change."

Research using a variety of theoretical frameworks and methodologies supported the claim that the frequency and quality of student-student and student-faculty interaction are most influential for college students' academic development, personal development, and satisfaction (Astin, 1993; Light, 1992; Johnson, Johnson, and Smith, 1991b). Astin's (1993) large-scale correlational study of what matters in college (involving 27,064 students at 309 baccalaureate-granting institutions) found that two environmental factors were by far the most predictive of positive change in college students' academic development, personal development, and satisfaction. These two factors—interaction among students and interaction between faculty and students—carried by far the largest weights and affected more general education outcomes than any other environmental variables studied, including the curriculum content factors. This result indicates that how students approach their general education and how the faculty actually deliver the curriculum is more important than the formal curriculum, that is, the content, collection, and sequence of courses. The assessment study by Light (1992) of Harvard students indicates that one of the crucial factors in the educational development of the undergraduate is the degree to which the student is actively engaged or involved in the undergraduate experience. Johnson, Johnson, and Smith (1991a) summarized meta-analysis results for randomized design field and laboratory studies of cooperative, competitive and individualistic learning and reported significant effect sizes for cooperative learning for academic success, quality of relationships, and psychological adjustment. Several follow-up reports have provided further support for cooperative learning (Johnson, Johnson, and Smith, 1998, 2007; Smith, Sheppard, Johnson, and Johnson, 2005; Springer, Stanne, and Donovan, 1999).

Emphasis on the importance of student engagement in learning continued in *NDTL* 67 and 74. Sutherland and Bonwell (1996) featured a broad range of faculty options for using active learning and college classes in *NDTL* 67, and Anderson and Speck (1998) argued that we need to change the way we grade student performance under the new learning paradigm.

I was delighted to see problem-based learning featured in *NDTL* 68, since it provided more support for student engagement and highlighted the role of structure and tasks. Many of the articles in this volume were salient for me; however, the opening paragraph of the concluding section continues to resonate with me: "Common to many of the stories in this issue is a complaint about the skills of university graduates. In business, education, science, architecture, and medicine, we are concerned to note that our graduates possess a knowledge base that is too theoretical and abstract, that they are out of touch with important problems of society or their discipline, and that they lack communication skills. Our authors have turned to problem-based learning (PBL) as one means of addressing these concerns. In a problem-based classroom, students are actively engaged in constructing knowledge and developing skills in using that knowledge for problem analysis and resolution through self-directed study and collaborative discussion" (Wilkerson and Gijselaers, 1996, p. 101). I, too, had turned to problem-based learning, and discovering that I was part of a larger community was reassuring.

A strong presence for learning communities emerged during this period, including *NDTL* 41 (Gabelnick and others, 1990), and this work has continued to flourish. A recent synthesis of this extraordinary work is *Learning Communities: Reforming Undergraduate Education* (Smith and others, 2004). Learning communities continue to be advocated as a "high impact educational practice" (Kuh, 2008), and I am confident that the prominence of learning communities will increase, and will have an enormous influence on students' personal and academic development as well as their sense of belonging.

NEW DIRECTIONS FOR TEACHING AND LEARNING • DOI: 10.1002/tl

The emphasis on the social basis of learning was maintained during the first decade of the twenty-first century, the third decade of *NDTL*. *Strategies for Energizing Large Classes: From Small Groups to Learning Communities* presented the stories of forty-eight instructors across the North American continent who are infusing their classes with small-group activities or are working explicitly to create student community within large classes (MacGregor, Cooper, Smith, and Robinson, 2000). A common response among the instructors who were interviewed was their surprise at our interest. They didn't think anyone was interested and they were frustrated that their colleagues didn't seem to care. They thought they were the only one, and as a result of *NDTL* 81 they discovered that there is a broader community of faculty who are committed to facilitating student learning in large classes.

Problem-based learning was revisited in 2003 in *NDTL* 95, and the editors (Knowlton and Sharp) addressed the role of PBL in the information age. Specifically, they provided articles that emphasized design and implementation issues, including philosophical and theoretical issues, integration of design and implementation, and implementation and facilitation.

One of the most research-intensive volumes that focused on the social basis of learning was *NDTL* 108, *Developing Student Expertise and Community: Lessons from How People Learn* (Petrosino, Martin, and Svihla, 2006), in which the authors describe results from a collaboration of learning scientists, assessment experts, learning technologists, and bioengineering domain experts who described a vision to transform bioengineering education to produce adaptive experts. McKenna (2006), "Implementing Learning—Science Research in University Settings: New Research Opportunities," highlighted the differences between K–12 teachers (where much of the learning science research is based) and university faculty and argued that because university faculty are predominantly subject-matter experts and few have training in learning methods and theories, there is a pressing need for learning science research.

Two recent volumes, *NDTL* 116 and 117, focused on the social basis of learning, one devoted to a very specific form of student engagement, team-based learning (Michaelson, Sweet, and Parmelee, 2008), and the other focused on improving the climate for undergraduate teaching and learning (Baldwin, 2009).

The social basis of learning is sufficiently developed and embraced by the higher educating community that there is a mushrooming of specific practices emerging—team-based learning (TBL), peer instruction (PI), process-oriented guided-inquiry learning (POGIL), just-in-time-teaching (JITT), and many more. Two of my favorites are the large-class implementation of PBL in undergraduate courses at the University of Delaware (Allen, Duch, and Groh, 1996), and student-centered active learning environment for undergraduate programs (SCALE-UP) (Beichner, 2006).

New Directions for Teaching and Learning 117 focused on science, mathematics, engineering, and technology (STEM) fields (Baldwin, 2009), fields that have lagged in embracing the social basis of learning. As noted in Table 2.1, 59% of faculty report that they use cooperative learning in all or most courses, and 17% reporting grading "on the curve." One indication of the lag is Astin's (1993) comparison of engineering faculty with all faculty. Astin reported that 43% of engineering faculty reported "grading 'on the curve,'" compared with 22% of all faculty. Sadly, many STEM faculty have not figured out that it is difficult, if not impossible, to get students to work together and help one another if they are pitted against one another by a competitive grading system (grading 'on the curve'). STEM disciplines are getting considerable attention, and one prominent example that is highly relevant for the social basis of learning is the Board of Science Education Workshop, Evidence on Promising Practices in Undergraduate Science, Technology, Engineering, and Mathematics (STEM) Education.

Fairweather (2008) argues in his summary report on the workshop, ". . . although faculty in STEM disciplines vary substantially on a broad array of attitudinal and behavioral measures" (Fairweather and Paulson, 2008) careful reviews of the substantial literature on college teaching and learning suggest that the pedagogical strategies most effective in enhancing student learning outcomes are not discipline dependent (Pascarella and Terenzini, 2005). Instead, active and collaborative instruction coupled with various means to encourage student engagement invariably lead to better student learning outcomes irrespective of academic discipline (Kuh, Kinzie, Schuh, and Witt, 2005; Kuh, Kinzie, Buckley, Bridges, and Kayek, 2007). The assumption that pedagogical effectiveness is disciplinary specific can result in "reinventing the wheel," proving yet again that pedagogies engaging students lead to better learning outcomes (2005, pp. 4 and 5).

Social Basis of Learning and the Future of *New Directions for Teaching and Learning*

What will the next thirty years bring and what role will *NDTL* play? There is strong agreement that it's impossible to predict the future; however, based on the history of *NDTL* and my experience as an author of several *NDTL* articles, it seems reasonable to speculate.

Svinicki (1990, p. 1) wrote, "There is a real need for 'translators and disseminators' whose job it is to extract the best from the array of potential ideas and pass it along in workable form to individual faculty members," and I think this will continue to be a crucial need and a role that *NDTL* will help fulfill. The challenges are great, however, as Fairweather (2008) argues. "Finally, resistance to adopting more effective teaching strategies in part derives from the perception of STEM faculty that the teaching process is at odds with the research process, and that research is more interesting and more valued at their institutions (Fairweather, 1996; Massy, Wilger, and Colbeck, 1994). The perception of the importance of teaching in faculty rewards and the perceived consequence of spending more time on improving teaching, namely having less time for research, adversely affects faculty involvement in pedagogical reform" (Fairweather, 2005). This behavioral pattern holds true even when faculty members express a deep commitment to teaching and to their students (Leslie, 2002).

I sincerely hope *NDTL* will continue to focus on the nexus between theory and practice and that more faculty will turn to *NDTL* for guidance in identifying and embracing evidence-based promising practices.

Thirty years have passed since I first encountered *NDTL* and I still eagerly open each issue as it arrives in anticipation of the new ideas and insights. A big part of my current work with graduate students and faculty (especially early-career faculty) is to help them develop a deep interest in and appreciation of the importance of connections between theory and practice, as is captured very well in *NDTL*. Best wishes with the transition. Keep up the terrific work.

References

Allen, D. E., Duch, B. J., and Groh, S. E. "The Power of Problem-Based Learning in Teaching Introductory Science Courses." In L. Wilkerson and W. H. Gijselaers (eds.), *Bringing Problem-Based Learning to Higher Education.* New Directions for Teaching and Learning, no. 68. San Francisco: Jossey-Bass, 1996.

Anderson, B., and Speck, B. W. (eds.). *Changing the Way We Grade Student Performance: Classroom Assessment and the New Learning Paradigm.* New Directions for Teaching and Learning, no. 74. San Francisco: Jossey-Bass, 1998.

Astin, A. *What Matters in College? Four Critical Years Revisited.* San Francisco: Jossey-Bass, 1993.

Astin, A. W. "Student Involvement: A Developmental Theory for Higher Education." *Journal of College Student Personnel*, 1984, 25, 297–308.

Axelrod, J. *The University Teacher as Artist.* San Francisco: Jossey-Bass, 1973.

Axelrod, J. "From Counterculture to Counterrevolution: A Teaching Career 1959–1984." In K. Eble (ed.), *Improving Teaching Styles.* New Directions for Teaching and Learning, no. 1. San Francisco: Jossey-Bass, 1980.

Baldwin, R. G. (ed.). *Improving the Climate for Undergraduate Teaching and Learning in STEM Fields.* New Directions for Teaching and Learning, no. 117. San Francisco: Jossey-Bass, 2009.

Barr, R. B., and Tagg, J. "From Teaching to Learning: A New Paradigm for Undergraduate Education." *Change*, 1995, 27(6), 12–25.

Beichner, R., (2006). "North Carolina State University: SCALE-UP." In D. Oblinger, (ed.), *Learning Spaces.* Boulder, CO: Educause.

Beichner, R. J., Saul, J. M., Abbott, D. S., Morse, J. J., Deardorff, D. L., Allain, R. J., Bonham, S. W., Dancy, M. H., and Risley, J. S. "The Student-Centered Activities for Large Enrollment Undergraduate Programs (SCALE-UP) Project." In E. F. Redish and P. J. Cooney (eds.), *Research-Based Reform of University Physics.* College Park, Md.: American Association of Physics Teachers, forthcoming.

Bonwell, C. C., and Sutherlund, T. E. (eds.). *Using Active Learning in College Classes: A Range of Options for Faculty.* New Directions for Teaching and Learning, no. 67. San Francisco: Jossey-Bass, 1996.

Bouton, C., and Rice, B. "Developing Student Skills and Abilities." New Directions for Teaching and Learning, no., 14 pp. 31–40. San Francisco: Jossey-Bass, 1983.

Campbell, W. E., and Smith, K. A. (eds.). 1997. *New paradigms for college teaching.* Edina, MN: Interaction Book Company.

Chickering, A. W., and Gamson, Z. F. "Seven Principles for Good Practice in Higher Education." *American Association for Higher Education Bulletin*, 1987, *39*, 3–7.

Colander, D. "The Art of Teaching Economics." *International Review of Economics Education*, 2004, *3*(1), 63–76.

Cooper, J. L., and Robinson, R. "The Argument for Making Large Classes Seem Small." In J. MacGregor, J. L. Cooper, K. A. Smith, and P. Robinson (eds.), *Strategies for Energizing Large Classes: From Small Groups to Learning Communities.* New Directions for Teaching and Learning, no. 81. San Francisco: Jossey-Bass, 2000.

DeAngelo, L., Hurtado, S., Pryor, J. H., Kelly, K. R., and Santos, J. L. (2009). *The American college teacher: National norms for the 2007-2008 HERI faculty survey.* Los Angeles: Higher Education Research Institute, UCLA.

Eble, K. (ed.). *Improving Teaching Styles.* New Directions for Teaching and Learning, no. 1. San Francisco: Jossey-Bass, 1980.

Fairweather, J. (1996). *Faculty work and public trust: Restoring the value of teaching and public service in American academic life.* Boston: Allyn & Bacon.

Fairweather, J. (2005). Beyond the Rhetoric: Trends in the Relative Value of Teaching and Research in Faculty Salaries. *Journal of Higher Education, 76*, 401–422.

Fairweather, J. (2008). "Linking Evidence and Promising Practices in Science, Technology, Engineering, and Mathematics (STEM) Undergraduate Education: A Status Report." Commissioned Paper for the Board of Science Education Workshop, Evidence on Promising Practices in Undergraduate Science, Technology, Engineering, and Mathematics (STEM) Education. [http://www7.nationalacademies.org/bose/PP_Commissioned_Papers.html]

Fairweather, J., and Paulson, K. "The Evolution of Scientific Fields in American Universities: Disciplinary Differences, Institutional Isomorphism." In J. Valimaa and O. Ylijoki (eds.), *Cultural Perspectives in Higher Education* (pp. 197–212). Dordrecht, Netherlands: Springer, 2008.

Finkel, D. L., and Monk, G. (1983). "Teachers and Learning Groups: Dissolution of the Atlas Complex." In C. Bouton and R. Y. Garth (eds.), *New Directions for Teaching and Learning, 14*, pp. 83–97.

Frederick, P. J. "Student Involvement: Active Learning in Large Classes." In M. G. Weimer (ed.), *Teaching Large Classes Well.* New Directions for Teaching and Learning, no. 32. San Francisco: Jossey-Bass, 1987.

Gabelnick, F., MacGregor, J., Matthews, R. S., and Smith, B. L (eds.). *Learning Communities: Creating Connections Among Students, Faculty, and Disciplines.* New Directions for Teaching and Learning, no. 41. San Francisco: Jossey-Bass, 1990.

Gamson, Z. F. (1991). A brief history of the seven principles for good practice in undergraduate education. In A. W. Chickering & Z. F. Gamson (eds.), *Applying the seven principles for good practice in undergraduate education. New Directions in Teaching and Learning*, no. 47 (pp. 5–12). San Francisco: Jossey-Bass.

Glassman, E. "The Teacher as Leader." In K. Eble (ed.), *Improving Teaching Styles.* New Directions for Teaching and Learning, no. 1. San Francisco: Jossey-Bass, 1980.

Johnson, D. W., Johnson, D. T., and Smith, K. A. *Active Learning: Cooperation in the College Classroom.* (1st ed.) Edina, Minn.: Interaction Book Co., 1991a.

Johnson, D. W., Johnson, R. T., and Smith, K. A. *Cooperative Learning: Increasing College Faculty Instructional Productivity.* ASHE-ERIC Report on Higher Education. Washington, D.C.: The George Washington University, 1991b.

Johnson, D. W., Johnson, R. T., and Smith, K. A. "Cooperative Learning Returns to College: What Evidence Is There That it Works?" *Change*, 1998, *30*(4), 26–35.

Johnson, D. W., Johnson, R. T., and Smith, K. A. "The State of Cooperative Learning in Postsecondary and Professional Settings." *Educational Psychology Review,* 2007, *19*(1), 15–29.

Kuh, G., Kinzie, J., Buckley, J., Bridges, B., and Kayek, J. *Piecing Together the Student Success Puzzle: Research, Propositions, and Recommendations.* Washington, D.C.: Association for the Study of Higher Education, 2007.

Kuh, G., Kinzie, J., Schuh, J., and Witt, E. *Student Success in College: Creating Conditions That Matter.* Washington, D.C.: Association for the Study of Higher Education, 2005.

Kuh, G. D. *High-Impact Educational Practices: What They Are, Who Has Access to Them, and Why They Matter.* Washington, D.C.: Association for American Colleges and Universities, 2008.

Leslie, D. "Resolving the Dispute: Teaching Is Academe's Core Value." *Journal of Higher Education,* 2002, *73,* 49–73.

Light, R. J. *The Harvard Assessment Seminars: Second Report.* Cambridge, Mass.: Harvard University Press, 1992.

MacGregor, J., Cooper, J., Smith, K., & Robinson, P. (2000). Strategies for energizing large classes: From small groups to learning communities. New Directions for Teaching and Learning vol. 81. San Francisco, Jossey-Bass.

Massy, W., Wilger, A., and Colbeck, C. "Department Cultures and Teaching Quality Overcoming 'Hallowed' Collegiality." *Change,* 1994, *26,* 11–20.

McKenna, A. (2006). Implementing learning-science research in university settings: New research opportunities. New Directions for Teaching and Learning vol. 108. San Francisco, Jossey-Bass.

McKeachie, W. J. "Improving Lectures by Understanding Students' Information Processing." In W. J. McKeachie (ed.), *Learning, Cognition, and College Teaching.* New Directions for Teaching and Learning, no. 2. San Francisco: Jossey-Bass, 1980.

Michaelson, L. K., Sweet, M., and Parmelee, D. X. *Team-Based Learning: Small-Group Learning's Next Big Step.* New Directions for Teaching and Learning, no. 116. San Francisco: Jossey-Bass, 2008.

National Institute of Education. *Involvement in Learning: Revitalizing Involvement in Learning: Realizing the Potential of American Higher Education. Final Report of the Study Group on the Conditions of Excellence in American Higher Education,* Washington, D.C., 1984.

Nelson Laird, T. F., Shoup, R., Kuh, G. D., and Schwarz, M. J. "The Effects of Discipline on Deep Approaches to Student Learning and College Outcomes." *Research in Higher Education,* 2008, *49,* 469–494.

Pascarella, E., and Terenzini, P. *How College Affects Students: A Third Decade of Research.* San Francisco: Jossey-Bass, 2005.

Pascarella, E. T., and Terenzini, P. T. *How College Affects Students: Findings and Insights from Twenty Years of Research.* San Francisco: Jossey-Bass, 1991.

Petrosino, A. J., Martin, T., and Svihla, V. *Developing Student Expertise and Community: Lessons from How People Learn.* New Directions for Teaching and Learning, no. 95. San Francisco: Jossey-Bass, 2006.

Smith, B. L., MacGregor, J., Matthews, R. S., and Gabelnick, F. *Learning Communities: Reforming Undergraduate Education.* San Francisco: Jossey-Bass, 2004.

Smith, K., and Waller, A. "Afterword: New Paradigms of College Teaching." In W. Cambell and K. Smith (eds.), *New Paradigms for College Teaching.* Edina, Minn.: Interaction Book Co., 1997.

Smith, K. A., Sheppard, S. D., Johnson, D. W., and Johnson, R. T. "Pedagogies of Engagement: Classroom-Based Practices." *Journal of Engineering Education,* 2005, *94*(1), 87–102.

Springer, L., Stanne, M. E., and Donovan, S. S. "Effect of Small Group Learning on Undergraduates in Science, Mathematics, Engineering and Technology: A Meta-Analysis." *Review of Educational Research*, 1999, *69*(1), 21–51.

Stanley, C. A., and Porter, M. E. *Engaging Large Classes: Strategies and Techniques for College Faculty.* San Francisco: Jossey-Bass, 2002.

Svinicki, M. D. "Editor's Notes." In M. D. Svinicki (ed.), *The Changing Face of College Teaching.* New Directions for Teaching and Learning, no. 42. San Francisco: Jossey-Bass, 1990.

Sutherland, T. E., and Bonwell, C. C (eds.) *Using Active Learning in College Classes: A Range of Options for Faculty.* New Directions for Teaching and Learning, vol. 67. San Francisco: Jossey-Bass, pp. 3–16.

Wilkerson, L., and Gijselaers, W. H. (eds.). *Bringing Problem-Based Learning to Higher Education.* New Directions for Teaching and Learning, no. 68. San Francisco: Jossey-Bass, 1996.

KARL A. SMITH is the cooperative learning professor of engineering education in the School of Engineering Education, at Purdue University West Lafayette. He has been at the University of Minnesota since 1972 and is in phased retirement as Morse-Alumni Distinguished Professor of Civil Engineering. Karl has worked with thousands of faculty all over the world on pedagogies of engagement, especially cooperative learning, problem-based learning, and constructive controversy. Please refer to his Web site for details—http://www.ce.umn .edu/~smith/. He has co-authored eight books, including How to Model It: Problem Solving for the Computer Age; Active Learning: Cooperation in the College Classroom (3rd ed.); Cooperative Learning: Increasing College Faculty Instructional Productivity; Strategies for Energizing Large Classes: From Small Groups to Learning Communities; *and* Teamwork and Project Management (3rd ed.).

NEW DIRECTIONS FOR TEACHING AND LEARNING • DOI: 10.1002/tl

3

Technology and its uses have undergone significant change in the past several decades. Technology has many benefits and it has impacted many of the ways that teaching and learning occur. However, the role of thoughtful consideration, selection, implementation, and assessment of the technology remains the ultimate responsibility of the teacher.

The Promise of Technology for College Instruction: From Drill and Practice to Avatars

Sally Kuhlenschmidt, Barbara Kacer

The specific tools and functions of technology have changed dramatically over the past half century, and have altered the face of postsecondary education. Key questions raised by the technological revolution include: Does technology drive us to teach differently? And if so, do we teach better or worse? Most importantly, what kind of impact has technology had on student learning?

Technology Circa 1960

The role of technology in the typical college classroom around 1960 was considerably more muted than today. The tools were supported delivery of course content, whether through displaying a lecturer's notes through an opaque projector or duplicating materials for distribution to students. Communication media, such as phones, were not commonly found inside a classroom, and computers were used by a relatively small segment of faculty, primarily for research. Distance learning, more likely known as correspondence studies, used the postal mail service, and only in some areas was radio or broadcast television used for sharing lessons. Technology did not have a prominent role in education or in educational philosophy. The content and the role of the instructor as sage on the stage were primary.

NEW DIRECTIONS FOR TEACHING AND LEARNING, no. 123, Fall 2010 © Wiley Periodicals, Inc.
View this article online at wileyonlinelibrary.com. • DOI: 10.1002/tl.406

The typical classroom in 1960 was likely to offer a chalkboard and perhaps an overhead projector. In 1960 the most elaborate version consisted of several boards that could be rolled on tracks to alternate the display. Another type allowed the instructor to flip the entire board so that the back side could be written upon. Some instructors used colored chalks to highlight different concepts. A felt eraser cleaned the board. One virtue of the chalkboard was that the instructor could write an outline of the lesson and the display remained for students to view throughout the class. A disadvantage was the chalk dust that covered clothes and fingers.

The overhead projector was developed by the United States Army for training large numbers of troops, and from there was gradually adopted by higher education. The projector shone a light through a flat surface on which a clear plastic transparency was laid. If the transparency had writing or printing on it, no light passed through. The image was reflected by a mirror placed above the surface and projected onto a wall or screen. Often the image was bright enough to be seen with room lights shining. The instructor could prepare images on transparent plastic in advance, or could write directly on the plastic transparencies during the class, reducing reliance on a chalkboard. The overhead projector enabled the instructor to face the class while teaching and have students prepare materials to share on the transparencies while class was in session. Color images could be displayed at higher cost.

Sixteen-millimeter film from the institutional film library was the typical way to show a video, although there was some market for 8-millimeter film, usually single-concept films. Running the projector required a modicum of skill, as the film could break or the sound could be out of sync. Producing a film required much skill; bulky, expensive equipment; and patience. Educational films were generally produced by businesses. Samples of films from this era are available on-line (Alexander, 2008; Internet Archive, n.d.).

College faculty were more likely to rely on slides from 35-mm cameras for sharing personal visual experiences of educational value. Slides displayed images fixed on a plastic transparency, about 1-inch square, and mounted in a cardboard frame. Slide projectors were used to shine a light through the transparency, projecting a strong beam onto a screen. Images could be obtained from companies that produced collections for educational purposes (for example, art or medical slides). There were few options for correcting a photo that was poorly done, and the results were not visible until the film was developed, days or weeks after the picture was taken. A university at most printed black and white photos in house. Color film had to be sent to a special lab. Each slide was individually slotted into a carousel, unique to a brand of slide projector, holding from 40–60 slides each. A common error was to put slides into the carousel upside down or backwards. An enthusiast could fill a wall with these bulky storage devices. Without strict adherence to an organizational scheme, locating a particular slide required setting up display equipment and viewing the slides one at a time, placing them against a light source.

The most recent innovation in audio was the reel-to-reel tape recorder using magnetic tape, followed by smaller audiocassette players in 1963. Tapes played over and over would begin to stretch and sound would degrade. The devices themselves were large and heavy. Long-play (LP) records were available as well.

Television was still relatively new (introduced at the 1939 World's Fair), and creative thinkers envisioned educational applications, but few applications had widespread impact in the college classroom. Only 17 programs in the United States were using television as part of their instruction in the late 1950s (Jeffries, n.d.). Only 50 colleges were using instructional television in 1961 (Cuban, 1986). The National Educational Television Network (NET) had 53 station affiliates by 1961 (Jeffries, n.d.). Documentaries developed for television would become useful in classrooms for institutions that could afford to buy public display rights. Before the era of cable television, having only three network channels provided a common culture for classroom examples.

In the course of preparing for a class the instructor or support staff may have used a mimeograph or spirit duplicator to make copies of materials for students. This entailed creating a master on a special type of paper, attaching the master to the machine's drum and turning a crank to pass paper through for printing. The copies had a distinct smell long remembered by persons who used them, and a tendency to turn fingers blue from the ink. The quality of reproduction varied as application of ink faded across copies.

Notes and handouts would have been either handwritten or created on manual typewriters. Disposable ink pens were relatively new on the market and prone to blot or skip. Manual typewriters required strength to strike the keys and leave a mark on the paper through the ribbon (which faded with use and had to be replaced). The 1950s saw the widespread adoption of electric typewriters, which required less force. Making corrections on typed documents was challenging, involving a special eraser, painting over the error with white ink or, in the later generations, using a correction tape or automatic correction. The error was visible on close inspection. Copies were made at the time of the original document by inserting carbon paper and a sheet of blank paper for every copy. The typist had to strike especially hard to have the image appear through the stack of pages.

If instructors wanted to contact a student they used a phone, physically connected by wire to the phone jack in their offices. There was only one phone company, which set prices as it wished. Long-distance numbers were especially costly. Or, the instructor could send a letter through the post office.

If instructors or students wanted to research a topic, they had to visit the library and physically look through the card catalog, a large collection of cards listing each book and resource in the library. The researcher wrote down the information from each card of interest, then went and located the book. They may also have used microfiche, miniaturized documents that were read with a special machine and that could slowly print poor copies. Material was almost exclusively produced through the auspices of a publishing house, after extensive editing, and it generally took at least a year, if not several years, to go from manuscript to published work.

The term *computer* had only recently come to mean the electronic digital calculator. (In the 1940s the word meant a person who performed calculations.) Computers circa 1960 consisted of multiple large pieces of equipment. That all the equipment fit in only one room was considered an advance. The year 1960 introduced the first computerized video game, a commercial modem for networking computers, and the COBOL language (Computer History Museum, 2008). Access was mostly limited to highly technical disciplines or business offices of the institution. Time on them was precious and paid for by the minute. Hand calculators were not available either, unless you count abacuses or slide rules. Large calculators that fit on a desk could be obtained but were quite expensive.

The launch of Sputnik increased interest in developing software specifically developed for classroom instruction, generally for precollege education. None truly caught on in the college classroom. (Years later general-purpose software, such as Microsoft Office, became the basis for instructional activities.) Simulations using technology were available in specialized fields, such as aeronautics and health care.

Programmed instruction (PI) was a dominant educational philosophy of the day, an approach strongly influenced by B. F. Skinner. Skinner and Holland first used PI in their behavioral psychology courses at Harvard in 1957 (Saettler, 1990). In 1958, Skinner created a teaching machine that provided small units of instruction based on behavioral objectives. The student responded to questions and received immediate feedback, then moved on to the next concept. Computer-assisted instruction (CAI) emerged in the 1960s and often consisted of drill-and-practice. In CAI, similar to PI, the emphasis was on immediate feedback, small steps, the student working at his/her own rate, and working until mastery of the material was achieved (Saettler, 1990).

The college classroom circa 1960 felt like a private community headed by the instructor. Students were separated from the world in order to learn in the ivory tower. The university was a place apart, and technology was not a particularly noteworthy part of that life.

Technology Circa 2010

Today, the teacher is bombarded by various forms of technology. The typical college classroom can only sample all of the options for sharing multimedia, producing and sharing materials, and communicating with others.

NEW DIRECTIONS FOR TEACHING AND LEARNING • DOI: 10.1002/tl

Clearly the computer revolution is at the heart of this change and has enabled a distance-learning explosion. Of course, using technology is not the challenge. The real challenge is using technology to advance student learning.

Today, we have to ask what the typical college classroom is. It may be a face-to-face classroom with four walls, a digital projector mounted from the ceiling, and a podium with a computer locked inside for showing PowerPoint slides. The classroom may have a white board or a "smart" board that records what the teacher inscribes for electronic sharing. The room may have a control panel with several different lighting and sound system selections. The teacher may use personal response systems or "clickers" to test student understanding immediately, display the collective class response, and provide immediate feedback to students. Or, the classroom may still be that 1960-era classroom with a chalkboard and an overhead projector. But the students arrive with cell phones and small computers, from programmable calculators to laptops to notebooks to e-book devices.

Or, today's typical college classroom may be an interactive television classroom with capacity to send the instruction around the world. It has one instructor teaching to multiple rooms of students, managing multiple cameras to capture the course; materials are displayed on a document camera.

Or, today's typical college classroom may not be a physical location. Entire programs are offered on-line, and learning is conducted through e-mail and course management systems, such as Blackboard, which combines on-line discussion, document delivery, and testing into one package. Video and audio may be selected from a wealth of material posted by the global community to YouTube (2005) or by teachers (TeacherTube, LLC, 2008), and content and interactive exercises can be found by searching the Web or depositories of instructional materials such as the Multimedia Educational Resource for Learning and Online Teaching (2009).

Available today with some effort is the felt experience of a classroom where none exists physically, by using a 3D virtual community, such as Second Life. Imagine a teacher able to share a virtual instructional environment (hospital? volcano? Supreme Court?) for students to explore on their own, experience lessons in simulations, and share those observations with others who have form and emotional expression as avatars.

Producing materials for instruction is incredibly easy. Digital cameras and editing software enable taking thousands of pictures, discarding what is not useful, and editing what is. Cheap video and audio equipment allow anyone to create videos, although a good video still requires skill to produce. Even easier is just using what others have shared on public depositories. Intellectual property has become increasingly complex as ownership takes on new meaning in an era of interactively produced documents. Even making print copies is simple with the wide availability of copy machines. Or one can send a document as an attachment in e-mail.

NEW DIRECTIONS FOR TEACHING AND LEARNING • DOI: 10.1002/tl

The Internet has made personal publishing ubiquitous, easy, and perhaps less thoughtful. New skills are required to tell what is trustworthy. The Internet has also made teaching public, even in the lowest-tech classroom, as students share their experiences in public places, such as profeval .com, Facebook, or Twitter. The products of teaching, such as syllabi, lecture notes, or video, are made trackable when they are digitized, and this contributes to possibilities for teaching accountability.

Government agencies, corporations, private citizens, and advocacy groups all publish their points of view to the Internet. The faculty role as "expert" is eroding. The wide availability of information and the ease of communication flattens the power curve, so college teachers may find their understanding challenged by students who visit Web sites during class. What remains is the role of guide to understanding.

With laptops and cell phones in the classroom, achieving a sheltered space for learning is difficult. There is no ivory tower. Students in the classroom are simultaneously engaged in their larger world, expecting to be connected to others whether via cell phone, Facebook, Twitter, or e-mail. With so many demands on their attention and access to well-produced stimuli from music to video, the teacher is challenged in creating a space for learning. In addition, the level of skill necessary for some types of instruction contributes to the disaggregation of teacher roles. Rather than being the center of all learning preparation, the instructor may be a "content expert," with others creating materials or managing the technology to deliver them. Or the instructor may be a learning facilitator, using material developed by others.

Computers in a variety of forms impact today's classrooms, from cell phones that are personal digital assistants to special-use tools such as health manikins. A less apparent but more powerful impact on education is the widespread use of databases. Databases allow users to rearrange information endlessly, connecting various data sets. Databases are felt at every level of university life, from the registrar's grade-tracking software to the basis for course management software, enabling management of ever larger numbers of students. Although specialized tools are relatively cheap to create and use, generic software, such as Microsoft Office, are widely integrated into today's teaching.

The Constructivist models of education are currently dominant, based on research on how the brain learns. Learners construct their understanding of the world and the educator provides core experiences and guides student interpretation. So what can we as teachers conclude from the impact of the technological revolution?

Lessons from Technology

Does technology drive us to teach differently? This can be answered in three ways: for the better, for the worse, and not at all.

NEW DIRECTIONS FOR TEACHING AND LEARNING • DOI: 10.1002/tl

Yes, Technology Has Influenced Teaching for the Better. Technology offers greater opportunities to give faster feedback to students, from clickers to e-mail. Today's tools permit more collaborative teaching via communication tools, and by flattening the power curve and reducing special claims of expertise by the teacher. Teachers and students can reach anyone, anywhere, anytime. Professional e-mail lists provide conversation regarding the latest thinking in a discipline and connect those interested in college teaching, increasing overall teaching scholarship. Technology also introduces competition. A university in a particular location can teach students anywhere. Technology removes privacy from teaching actions and thus increases teacher accountability. One example is the Quality Matters peer review of on-line course design, similar to research peer review (MarylandOnline, 2006).

Yes, Technology Has Made Teaching Worse. Today's toys compete with education for student attention. There is no protected environment for deeply engaging with material. In addition, PowerPoint encourages transmission of simple information and not higher levels of thinking. Other faculty use technology to distance themselves from student needs, replacing contact with the computer and possibly undermining student motivation for learning. Still others engage in "technology of the month"—changing techniques so often they fail to build expertise or think critically about uses of the tool.

When old technologies disappear, so too do some possibilities. A newer computer system may not run an older software, and skills developed in teaching with an older tool must be relearned with the latest incarnation, taking time away from students.

No, Technology Has Not Had a Noticeable Impact on Learning. Technology enables potential learning, but how a tool is used is more critical than the tool itself (Russell, 2001). Research on the potential impact of a technology requires time to derive results and interpret them, but technology changes before research can fully evaluate the impact. The basic learning tool (the brain) has not changed; thus teaching involves meeting the same issues as before the technology revolution.

We have had fifty years of research on human learning suggesting that constructivism and engagement play a central role in learning. Unfortunately, many of the technologies touted today replicate lecturing, whether delivering information in an asynchronous, distributed format (for example, podcasting) or face-to-face (for example, PowerPoint slides).

Has Technology Had an Impact on Student Learning?

Certainly technology can provide novelty and novelty grabs attention. And technology makes many tasks more efficient. However, applying technology in a manner that effectively improves learning is challenging as is evaluating whether the tool fits the situation. Because of rapidly changing technology, scientifically evaluating the impact of a tool on learning is particularly challenging. Russell (2001) completed a massive survey of research on the impact of different technological methods on instruction and has concluded that there is no significant difference in student outcomes between various modes of delivery. Perhaps this means we are free to choose among the options to satisfy the needs of a particular group of students. Or we may have simply carried over traditional ways of working with students and thus the underlying instruction has not shifted, despite having a new technology.

Conclusion

What *is* the promise of technology? Although the technology of 2010 has changed in ways unimaginable in 1960, the promise of technology today is similar to the promise of technology then. The achievement of student learning seems more likely to lie in the minds of the people who use the technology and in how they implement the tool rather than in some inherent quality of the tool. Although each generation promises that this new tool will increase efficiency of teaching and improve student learning, the reality is that learning is a human process. Technology can enable more possibilities. Technology can remove some barriers to learning (even as new barriers are introduced) and can provide real-world in-course experience to the extent the discipline in question relies on technology. Technology can enable more efficient communication (which begs the question of its worth). Technology can reduce or transfer to the tool some of the tedious tasks involved in education. The novelty of a technological tool can focus student attention for at least a while. Technology does not, however, release the humans in the equation (teachers and students) from responsibility for thoughtful consideration, selection, implementation, and assessment of the technology, or from ultimate responsibility for success in the learning process.

References

Alexander, G. "View Our Films." [http://www.afana.org/watchfilms.htm]. 2008.
Computer History Museum. "Timeline of Computer History." [http://www.computer-history.org/timeline/?year=1960]. 2008.
Cuban, L. *Teachers and Machines: The Classroom Use of Technology Since 1920.* New York: Teachers College Press, 1986.
Internet Archive. "Moving Image Archive." [http://www.archive.org/details/movies]. n.d.
Jeffries, M. "Research in Distance Education: The History of Distance Education." [http://www.digitalschool.net/edu/DL_history_mJeffries.html]. n.d.
MarylandOnline. "Quality Matters: Inter-institutional Quality Assurance in Online Learning." [http://www.digitalschool.net/edu/DL_history_mJeffries.html]. 2006.
Multimedia Educational Resource for Learning and Online Teaching. [http://www.merlot.org/merlot/] 2009.

Russell, T. *The No Significant Difference Phenomenon.* Raleigh, NC: North Carolina State University, 2001. [http://www.nosignificantdifference.org/].

Saettler, P. *The Evolution of American Educational Technology.* Englewood, CO: Libraries Unlimited, 1990.

TeacherTube, LLC. "TeacherTube: Teach the World." [http://www.teachertube.com/ 2008]. 2008.

YouTube, Inc. "YouTube." [http://www.youtube.com/]. 2005.

SALLY KUHLENSCHMIDT is a professor of psychology and director of the Faculty Center for Excellence in Teaching at Western Kentucky University. She has taught since 1986, including on-line, interactive video, and face-to-face courses. Her doctorate is from Purdue University in clinical psychology, and she has earned two on-line certificates (in Distance Education and Distance Education Certified Trainer) from the University of West Georgia. She has been director since 1994, and during that time has served on the board of the Professional and Organizational Development Network in Higher Education and recently was honored with the Spirit of POD Award and the Menges Award for Outstanding Research in Educational Development.

BARBARA KACER is an associate professor in the School of Teacher Education at Western Kentucky University. She is also the faculty associate at the Faculty Center for Excellence in Teaching. Her doctorate is from The University of Iowa in Instructional Design and Technology, and she has taught at WKU since 1989, including on-line, interactive video, and face-to-face courses. Dr. Kacer has worked in the area of multicultural education since the early 1990s.

4

Community-based learning is now more than a variation on community service. It is now a powerful pedagogy that can be used to enhance the common good. This pedagogy has proven itself to be an educational resource whose time has come.

Two Decades of Community-Based Learning

Edward Zlotkowski, Donna Duffy

In March of 2009, thirty-two individuals from higher education as well as the corporate and nonprofit sectors met in what the event's organizer, Richard Freeland, Jane and William Mosakowski Distinguished Professor of Higher Education at Clark University and Commissioner of Higher Education for Massachusetts, described as an "extended seminar." According to Freeland, the seminar's focus was the relationship between "learning experiences . . . predominantly academic exercises in traditional classroom settings" and long-term goals such as "preparing engaged citizens, effective professionals, and, more broadly, adults equipped to make significant contributions to society" (Freeland, 2009b). From a more exclusively pedagogical perspective, one could characterize the event as investigating the role of action-based, off-campus experiences in developing liberally educated individuals—the kinds of individuals one traditionally associates with a liberal arts education. Hence one of its primary sponsors was, quite appropriately, the American Association of Colleges and Universities (AAC&U). As the association's president, Carol Geary Schneider, noted (2009): "a good liberal education should take pride in preparing students for 'effective practice.' And how well it actually does that needs to become one of the hallmarks of excellence in this new global century."

Such an "establishment" that covens around and recognizes the potential academic significance of experiences that had until fairly recently been regarded as peripheral to "real" learning has great significance. Indeed, Freeland himself has called such a yoking of traditional academic

NEW DIRECTIONS FOR TEACHING AND LEARNING, no. 123, Fall 2010 © Wiley Periodicals, Inc.
View this article online at wileyonlinelibrary.com. • DOI: 10.1002/tl.407

concerns to effective practice a "necessary revolution" (2009a) because it challenges long-held assumptions about both the dominance and the sufficiency of purely conceptual classroom-centered learning. Furthermore, in calling for a reassessment of the role that contextualized learning experiences and unstructured problem solving could and should play in undergraduate education, the seminar participants took an important step toward acknowledging that the gap between what cognitive science and empirical research tell us about effective teaching and learning, and what actually happens in most academic programs, must be closed.

Although the Clark seminar was not focused specifically on community-based learning, it provides an excellent introduction to the latter for two interrelated reasons. First, as Freeland himself notes,

> The most prominent attempt to introduce practical activity into liberal education is the civic engagement movement, through which students are encouraged to participate in off-campus community service, sometimes in connection with credit-bearing service-learning courses, sometimes outside the formal curriculum. (Freeland, 2009a)

Second, precisely because the civic engagement movement, or more specifically, the pedagogical strategy most often referred to as service-learning, has played such a prominent role in raising the kinds of issues the Clark seminar explored, it is impossible to trace the recent history of community-based teaching and learning without understanding its symbiotic relationship to a broader set of developments in the contemporary academy.

To appreciate the importance of this relationship, one need look no further than Don Hill's "*Death of a Dream* Service Learning 1994–2010: A Historical Analysis by One of the Dreamers" (Hill, 1998). In this piece, Hill, at the time a member of the Service Learning 2000 Center at Stanford, offers ten (although the text reads "11") "distinct but related reasons" why by the year 2010 one will be able to pronounce service-learning "unofficially dead" (p. 1). To be sure, Hill's focus is K–12 education, not higher education. Nevertheless, it is not difficult to adapt almost all of his reasons to an academic context. This is especially true of his first reason, namely, "*Service learning never became an appealing possible classroom strategy to 'mainstream' teachers*" (original emphasis) (p. 1). This item goes on to explain that for too long "[s]ervice learning looked and smelled like an add-on fad that would in all due time pass from the scene" (pp. 1 and 29).

But in higher education this in fact did not happen, though it might well have, for the mid-1990s—probably just when Hill was writing his article—turned out to be a pivotal period for academic service-learning. Thanks to Campus Compact organizing, Ford Foundation funding, and a persuasive position paper written by Stanton (1990), then acting director of Stanford's Haas Center for Public Service, the first half of the decade saw an increasing focus on the faculty role in community-based work. Faculty, Stanton noted, had an essential role to play "in supporting student service efforts" (Stanton, 1990, p. 1). Indeed, without their participation it was unlikely the current service movement would ever gain traction.

But what exactly should faculty do? How should they utilize their now acknowledged importance? Some faculty, strongly motivated by social values and a commitment to underserved populations, believed it would be better for service-learning to remain the fringe phenomenon Hill describes rather than risk sacrificing its social efficacy to more academic ends. Another group argued that nothing in the long run could be achieved unless a way was found to lend community-based work the academic legitimacy that would broaden its appeal. It was the work of this second group that helped usher in a new stage in the development of the civic engagement movement, a stage characterized by intensive resource development, especially in and through the academic disciplines and their national and regional associations.

Probably the single most visible manifestation of this new interest in academic resource building was what eventually became the American Association for Higher Education's twenty-one-volume series on service-learning in the academic disciplines (Zlotkowski, 1997–2006). However, that series was quickly complemented by a host of other discipline- and institutional-type specific resources (Zlotkowski, 2000, 2001, 2005). Because more than half of Hill's ten reasons for service-learning's projected decline involve some kind of failure to develop resources or support structures, this surge of activity effectively served to save service-learning in higher education from the decline Hill predicted for K–12 programs. Indeed, over the years that followed more than one service-learning proponent has felt compelled to caution that academic values and interests may, if anything, be too much in evidence, thereby eclipsing other social and civic concerns and undermining the principle of academy-community reciprocity (Harkavy, 2000; Saltmarsh and Hartley, forthcoming).

But it was not just charges of social and/or civic neglect that a rapidly developing civic engagement movement had to contend with. As community-based work became more popular with college and university faculty with each passing year, it came under increasing pressure to demonstrate its effectiveness, especially its academic effectiveness. A new academic journal, the *Michigan Journal of Community Service Learning*, helped meet this demand with peer-reviewed articles on, among other things, the assessment of learning outcomes in service-learning courses and programs. At the same time, the Higher Education Research Institute (HERI) at UCLA began to take an interest in assessing service-learning's contribution to student growth in all areas—academic, personal, and civic—and reported promising results (see, for example, Astin, 2000). Finally, in 1999 Eyler and Giles (1999), faculty researchers at Vanderbilt University's Peabody College of Education and Human Development, published their *Where's the*

Learning in Service-Learning? Based on an extensive qualitative and quantitative research, the book made it clear that, implemented in a thorough and skillful manner, service-learning was indeed a "powerful pedagogy," able to contribute substantially to student growth in a wide variety of ways.

By this point, service-learning was poised to enter the growing national conversation on what constituted appropriate educational methodology in general. A decade earlier Chickering and Gamson (1987) had formulated seven principles for good practice in undergraduate education focusing on processes that support learning across all content areas. Discussion about these principles encouraged faculty to recognize that teaching involves more than having proficiency in a subject area and led to campus conversations regarding what is needed for truly effective teaching. Angelo (1993) proposed fourteen principles that focus on how learning takes place in the classroom, and the American Psychological Association (1997) formulated a set of fourteen learner-centered psychological principles. The first of these learner-centered principles states that "successful learners are active, goal-directed, self-regulating, and assume personal responsibility for contributing to their own learning" (American Psychological Association, 1997, p. 3). The disconnect between viewing successful learners as necessarily active while acknowledging the passive setting of most college classrooms is clearly articulated in the Barr and Tagg (1995) influential call for a paradigm shift from teaching to learning. Their article set the stage for major changes in higher education from administrative procedures to classroom practices to assessment of student learning outcomes. The current focus on student success echoes their suggestion that "the faculty and the institution take an R. Buckminster Fuller view of students: human beings are born geniuses and designed for success. If they fail to display their genius or fail to succeed, it is because their design function is being thwarted" (Barr and Tagg, 1995, p. 23).

The Commission on Behavioral and Social Sciences and Education of the National Research Council addressed the challenges of understanding the design function of learning in its book, *How People Learn: Brain, Mind, Experience and School* (Bransford, Brown, and Cocking, 2000). Studies support the importance of helping students to think more like experts in a field and suggest that "transfer across contexts is especially difficult when a subject is taught only in a single context rather than in multiple contexts" (p. 62). Here, as also in the case of all the other studies just cited, service-learning aligns effectively with the guidelines proposed. Students participate in community settings with different types of experts, and they reflect on how course concepts fit into a range of contexts.

Of special relevance in this regard is the work of Halpern and Hakel (2003), who emphasize the importance of applying empirically based research to find ways to enhance the transfer of learning from the classroom to other settings. Their principle that "varying the conditions under which learning takes place makes learning harder for learners but results in better learning" (p. 39) can be seen in service-learning settings when students struggle to understand why a clear-cut concept from their textbooks is hard to recognize in the complicated environment of a preschool classroom or homeless shelter. Another of the Halpern and Hakel principles, namely, that "experience alone is a poor teacher" (p. 40), serves as a key reminder of the importance of preparing students adequately for a service-learning experience and ensuring that ongoing reflection is central to the process. Students need to assess their background knowledge as they begin a project and monitor how it may change over time. As Halpern and Hakel state, "what professors do in their classes matters far less than what they ask *students* to do" (p. 41).

This shift from an instructional to a learning focus has also led to new conceptualizations of how to define and assess what actually happens on college campuses. The National Survey on Student Engagement (NSSE), begun in 1998, has sparked widespread interest in the ways in which students are involved in activities both in and outside of the classroom. Shulman (2002) has proposed a "new table of learning"—with engagement and motivation, knowledge and understanding, performance and action, reflection and critique, judgment and design, and commitment and identity as key elements. He recommends that these elements serve as heuristics, as a language for playing with ideas about learning in students and institutions. Wiggins and McTighe (1998) and Fink (2003) have also created taxonomies for learning and have proposed concrete ways to design courses in order to address more holistic models of how people learn. Huber and Hutchings (2005) note that "the need for students to understand their own learning—to 'go meta'—is increasingly on higher education's radar screen" (p. 113).

Similarly, more faculty are "going meta" in examining how students learn through the scholarship of teaching and learning. They are exploring the kinds of conditions that help students move beyond superficial facts to a deeper understanding of subject matter. Perkins (1998) describes understanding as the ability "to perform flexibly with the topic—to explain, justify, extrapolate, relate and apply in ways that go beyond knowledge and routine skill. Understanding is a matter of being able to think and act flexibly with what you know" (p. 42). Taking the risk of venturing into an unknown community setting is one kind of activity that gives students this kind of opportunity "to perform flexibly with a topic." Because there are few "right" answers in responding to community settings, students have to make inquiries, try multiple solutions, and persevere. Such an option may be especially important for learners who are less successful in dealing with the structures of a traditional classroom environment, where the skill of performing flexibly may not be assessed or valued (Duffy, 2000, 2004). Hence it is not surprising that Kuh (2008) cites service-learning as one of the ten high-impact educational practices effective in increasing student engagement and retention—issues of critical importance on most campuses today. Similarly, Bean and Eaton (2002) list service-learning as one of the approaches that correspond to their psychological theory of retention, and Simonet (2008) demonstrates the ways in which service-learning connects to behavioral, cognitive, emotional, and social frameworks of engagement.

Academics exploring questions related to student learning focus closely on how, when, and why students do or do not "get" concepts within certain learning contexts. Tagg suggests that

> we have to see that learning—deep learning, learning that matters, learning that lasts—is not something that instructors do to students or even that students do for themselves. Rather, it is the product of action in a context shaped by goals, performance, feedback, time horizon, and community—all of the principles that define the cognitive economy, acting to create an environment that empowers and engages students. (Tagg, 2003, p. 322)

Creating such contexts for learning and self-authorship is the theme of Baxter Magolda's book on constructive-developmental pedagogy. She states that "self-authorship is impossible unless students are able to connect learning with their lived experiences; self-authorship requires making meaning of one's own experience" (Baxter Magolda, 1999, p. 13). As students reflect on their experiences in various community settings, they need to struggle to make sense of their experience when what they see and hear does not fit in with their existing worldview. This necessary adjustment may then prompt them to a new visioning of reality. A recent book by Werder and Otis (2010) expands on the importance of self-authorship and provides concrete examples—including service-learning examples—of ways in which students and faculty can collaboratively engage in collaborative meaning making and together discover the types of settings that engender significant learning experiences.

However, it is not just with regard to self-authorship and ownership of the learning process that service-learning has something important to offer in the area of student efficacy. Over the past few years, more and more service-learning programs have been experimenting with new forms of student academic leadership. In 2006 Campus Compact published *Students as Colleagues: Expanding the Circle of Service-Learning Leadership* (Zlotkowski, Longo, and Williams, 2006), an edited volume containing several dozen examples of programs in which students play key organizing, facilitating, and knowledge-generating roles. In these roles students often work alongside faculty and professional staff more as colleagues than as subordinates, hence the title *Students as Colleagues*.

Just as discipline-specific service-learning represented a logical extension of the more generic approaches to community-based work that had prevailed until the mid-1990s, so students as colleagues represent a logical

NEW DIRECTIONS FOR TEACHING AND LEARNING • DOI: 10.1002/tl

extension of the active learning emphasis inherent in the very nature of this approach to teaching and learning. As Bunn, Elansary, and Bowman (2006)—a student-staff collaborative team—write in "Penn's West Philadelphia Partnerships: Developing Students as Catalysts and Colleagues":

> . . . service-learning is a pedagogy that emphasizes democratic development . . . and thus is a natural fit with a course that employs a democratic learning process from course creation through implementation. The goals of both service-learning and democratic development are met to a greater extent when the two are employed together in the same course than when employed individually. (Bunn, Elansary, and Bowman, 2006, pp. 199–200)

To be sure, not all service-learning courses and programs utilize students in this manner, and for the foreseeable future, the concept will probably remain more exceptional than normative. Still, it offers still another indication of the way in which service-learning continues to anticipate and contribute to important new trends in the scholarship of teaching and learning.

There remains one other aspect of community-based work that deserves to be recognized as a possible harbinger of broader concerns. One of the most detailed, empirically grounded contributions to the Clark seminar was a paper by Robert Sternberg, Dean of the School of Arts and Sciences at Tufts University. Sternberg, a former president of the American Psychological Association, has developed a tripartite understanding of intelligence that places creative and practical abilities on a par with the analytical skills so long privileged by academics (Sternberg, 1985; Sternberg, 1997). In his Clark paper, Sternberg rehearses concepts and examples (already familiar to readers acquainted with Sternberg and Grigorenko, 2002) that clarify why traditional analytical skills, when developed to the exclusion of creative and practical skills, hardly presage professional success, whether inside or outside the academy. It is the examples under "teaching practically" that should especially draw our attention, for they consist primarily of the *kinds* of experiences routinely offered in service-learning courses: planning for a financial problem created by changing life circumstances, using a foreign language in the field, implementing a business plan, adapting an architectural design to specific environmental circumstances.

And yet, as compelling as these examples are in arguing for the merits of community-based teaching and learning, it is Sternberg's (2009) discussion of what he calls "wisdom" that adds something of special significance to our understanding of this approach. For up until now our discussion has focused almost exclusively on the academic and the cognitive. And yet, one could argue that what makes service-learning truly distinctive is its elevation of the civic to a place of equal importance. Indeed, when one reviews what George Kuh has called the "high impact practices" most relevant to the Clark seminar (Freeland, 2009b)—study abroad, undergraduate research, internships, co-op placements, and service-learning opportunities—it is primarily service-learning that insists upon the importance of civic learning, civic awareness, and civic experiences. And although many of the learning benefits we have identified can be effectively delivered through a variety of pedagogical approaches, the same cannot be said for civic development.

It is not unusual for service-learning advocates to encounter polite stares when they turn directly to this subject. To be sure, faculty increasingly recognize the importance of civic development within the overall frame of undergraduate education. Some are even willing to concede their own responsibility for contributing to this development. Nevertheless, the civic remains by and large one of the least well developed features of service-learning programs and community-based work (Colby and others, 2003; Saltmarsh and Hartley, forthcoming). Far too often it is seen as an add-on or perhaps an ideal rather than an essential feature of community-based work. Therein lies the significance of Sternberg's (2009) identification of wisdom—a quality that "builds on but goes beyond intelligence and creativity" (p. 2)—as "the most important attribute to seek in future citizens and professionals" (p. 20).

For what Sternberg understands by this concept is something very close to what service-learning advocates might call civic vision:

> A person could be practically intelligent, but use his or her practical intelligence toward bad or selfish ends. In wisdom, one certainly may seek good ends for oneself, but one also seeks common good outcomes for others. If one's motivations are to maximize certain people's interests and minimize other people's, wisdom is not involved. In wisdom, one seeks a common good, realizing that this common good may be better for some than for others. (p. 22)

From a variation on community service to a discipline-specific strategy to a powerful pedagogy to a vehicle of democracy and the common good, community-based learning has proven itself to be an educational resource whose time has come.

References

American Psychological Association. *Learner-Centered Psychological Principles: Guidelines for School Redesign and Reform.* Washington, D.C.: American Psychological Association, 1997.

Angelo, T. A. "A 'Teacher's Dozen': Fourteen General, Research-Based Principles for Improving Higher Learning in Our Classrooms." *American Association for Higher Education Bulletin*, 1993, *45*(8), 3–7.

Astin, A. W., Vogelgesang, L. J., Ikeda, E. K., and Yee, J. E. *How Service Learning Affects Students.* Los Angeles: Higher Education Research Institute, University of California, Los Angeles, 2000.

Barr, R. B., and Tagg, J. "From Teaching to Learning—A New Paradigm for Undergraduate Education." *Change,* 1995, 27(6), 12–25.

Baxter Magolda, M. B. *Creating Contexts for Learning and Self-Authorship.* Nashville: Vanderbilt University Press, 1999.

Bean, J., and Eaton, S. E. "The Psychology Underlying Successful Retention Practices." *Journal of College Student Retention,* 2002, 3(1), 73–89.

Bransford, J. D., Brown, A. L., and Cocking, R. R. (eds.). *How People Learn: Brain, Mind, Experience, and School.* Washington, D.C.: National Research Council, Committee on Developments in the Science of Learning, National Academy Press, 2000.

Bunn, J., Elansary, M., and Bowman, C. "Penn's West Philadelphia Partnerships: Developing Students as Catalysts and Colleagues." In E. Zlotkowski, N. V. Longo, and J. R. Williams (eds.), *Students as Colleagues: Expanding the Circle of Service-Learning Leadership.* Providence, R.I.: Campus Compact, 2006.

Chickering, A. W., and Gamson, Z. F. "Seven Principles for Good Practice in Undergraduate Education." *American Association for Higher Education Bulletin,* 1987, 39(7), 3–7.

Colby, A., Ehrlich, T., Beaumont, E., and Stephens, J. *Educating Citizens: Preparing America's Undergraduates for Lives of Moral and Civic Responsibility.* San Francisco: Jossey-Bass, 2003.

Duffy, D. K. "Resilient Students, Resilient Communities." In P. Hutchings (ed.), *Opening Lines: Approaches to the Scholarship of Teaching and Learning.* Palo Alto, Calif.: Carnegie Foundation for the Advancement of Teaching, 2000.

Duffy, D. K. "Service-Learning, Resilience, and Community: The Challenges of Authentic Assessment." In D. S. Dunn, C. M. Mehrotra, and J. S. Halonen (eds.), *Measuring Up: Educational Assessment Challenges and Practices for Psychology.* Washington, D.C.: American Psychological Association, 2004.

Eyler, J., and Giles, D. E., Jr. *Where's the Learning in Service-Learning?* San Francisco: Jossey-Bass, 1999.

Fink, L. D. *Creating Significant Learning Experiences: An Integrated Approach to Designing College Courses.* San Francisco: Jossey-Bass, 2003.

Freeland, R. M. "Liberal Education and Effective Practice: The Necessary Revolution in Undergraduate Education." *Liberal Education,* 2009a, 95(1). [http://www.aacu.org/liberaleducation/index.cfm].

Freeland, R. M. "The Clark/AAC&U Conference on Liberal Education and Effective Practice." *Liberal Education,* 2009b, 95(4). [http://www.aacu.org/liberaleducation/index.cfm].

Halpern, D. F., and Hakel, M. D. "Applying the Science of Learning to the University and Beyond." *Change,* 2003, 35(4), 36–41.

Harkavy, I. "Service-Learning, Academically Based Community Service, and the Historic Mission of the American Urban Research University." In I. Harkavy and B. M. Donovan (eds.), *Connecting Past and Present: Concepts and Models for Service-Learning in History.* Washington, D.C.: American Association for Higher Education, 2000.

Hill, D. "Death of a Dream Service Learning 1994–2010: A Historical Analysis by One of the Dreamers." *NSEE Quarterly,* 1998, 24(1), 1–31.

Huber, M. T., and Hutchings, P. *The Advancement of Learning: Building the Teaching Commons.* San Francisco: Jossey-Bass, 2005.

Kuh, G. D. "High-Impact Educational Practices." Excerpt from G. D. Kuh, *High-Impact Educational Practices: What They Are, Who Has Access to Them and Why They Matter.* Washington, D.C.: AAC&U, 2008. [https://www.aacu.org/leap/hip.cfm].

Perkins, D. "What is Understanding?" In M. S. Wiske (ed.), *Teaching for Understanding: Linking Research with Practice.* San Francisco: Jossey-Bass, 1998.

Saltmarsh, J., and Hartley, M. "Democratic Civic Engagement." In J. Saltmarsh and M. Hartley (eds.), *Higher Education and Democracy: The Future of Engagement.* Philadelphia, Pa.: Temple University Press, forthcoming.

Schneider, C. G. "The Clark/AAC&U Challenge: Connecting Liberal Education with Real-World Practice." *Liberal Education*, 2009, *95*(4). [http://www.aacu.org/liberaleducation/index.cfm].

Shulman, L. S. "Making Differences: A Table of Learning." *Change*, 2002, *34*(6), 36–44.

Simonet, D. "Service-Learning and Academic Success: The Links to Retention Research." *Minnesota Campus Compact*, May 2008. [http://www.mncampuscompact.org/].

Stanton, T. K. *Integrating Public Service with Academic Study: The Faculty Role.* Providence, R.I.: Campus Compact, 1990.

Sternberg, R. J. "Academic Intelligence Is Not Enough! WICS: An Expanded Model for Effective Practice in School and in Later Life." A paper commissioned for the conference on Liberal Education and Effective Practice, March 12–13, 2009. [http://www.clarku.edu/aboutclark/leep.cfm].

Sternberg, R. J. *Beyond IQ: A Triarchic Theory of Human Intelligence.* New York: Cambridge University Press, 1985.

Sternberg, R. J. *Successful Intelligence.* New York: Plume, 1997.

Sternberg, R. J., and Grigorenko, E. L. "The Theory of Successful Intelligence as a Basis for Instruction and Assessment in Higher Education." In D. F. Halpern and M. D. Hakel (eds.), *Applying the Science of Learning to University Teaching and Beyond.* New Directions for Teaching and Learning, no. 89. San Francisco: Jossey-Bass, 2002.

Tagg, J. *The Learning Paradigm College.* Bolton, Mass.: Anker, 2003.

Werder, C., and Otis, M. M. (eds.). *Engaging Student Voices in the Study of Teaching and Learning.* Sterling, Va.: Stylus, 2010.

Wiggins, G., and McTighe, J. *Understanding by Design.* Alexandria, Va.: Association for Supervision and Curriculum Development, 1998.

Zlotkowski, E. (series ed.). *Service-Learning in the Academic Disciplines.* Washington, D.C.: American Association for Higher Education, 1997–2006.

Zlotkowski, E. "Civic Engagement and the Academic Disciplines." In T. Ehrlich (ed.), *Civic Responsibility and Higher Education.* Phoenix: Oryx Press, 2000.

Zlotkowski, E. "Mapping New Terrain: Service-Learning Across the Disciplines." *Change*, 2001, *33*(1), 25–33.

Zlotkowski, E. "The Disciplines and the Public Good." In T. Chambers, A. Kezar, and J. Burkhardt (eds.), *Higher Education for the Public Good: Emerging Voices from a National Movement.* San Francisco: Jossey-Bass, 2005.

Zlotkowski, E., Longo, N. V., and Williams, J. R. (eds.). *Students as Colleagues: Expanding the Circle of Service-Learning Leadership.* Providence, R.I.: Campus Compact, 2006.

EDWARD ZLOTKOWSKI is a professor of English at Bentley College and in 1990 founded the Bentley Service-Learning Center. He received his B.A. in English and his Ph.D. in Comparative Literature from Yale University. He writes and speaks extensively on a wide range of service-learning and engagement-related topics, and served as general editor of the American Association for Higher Education's 21-volume series on service-learning in the academic disciplines. He also served as editor of Successful Service-Learning Programs, *published by Anker in 1998,* Service-Learning and the First-Year Experience, *published by the University of South Carolina in 2002, and as co-editor of* Students as Colleagues: Expanding the Circle of Service-Learning Leadership, *published by Campus Compact in 2006. A collection of his essays will be published in 2010 by Temple University Press. Dr. Zlotkowski is a senior associate at the New England Resource Center for Higher Education.*

DONNA DUFFY is professor of psychology and coordinator of the Carnegie Academy for the Scholarship of Teaching and Learning at Middlesex Community College, Bedford and Lowell, Massachusetts. She is the coauthor, with Janet Wright Jones, of Teaching Within the Rhythms of the Semester, *and the coeditor, with Robert Bringle, of* With Service in Mind, *a monograph on service-learning and psychology. She earned her doctorate from Washington University and received the Thomas Ehrlich Faculty Award for Service-Learning in 1999 for her work connecting service in the community to student learning in classrooms.*

5

Assessing learning in higher education can be a very difficult task. There are some differences, however, when assessing for accountability to others and assessing for transformation. These distinctions are embedded in our historical understanding of teaching and learning.

Assessing Learning: From Accountability to Transformation

Catherine M. Wehlburg

How do we know that learning has occurred? The simple answer is that we look to see if there has been some type of change in what a student can do. Evaluation of learning, in practice, however, is much more complex. Learning isn't always a clearly defined change in behavior. In some areas of learning we can look for this behavior change: a student cannot read the word *book*, but after several trials and attempts for which he or she gets feedback, the student now can. But as we move into higher education and more complex levels of learning, measuring learning isn't easy. And it doesn't always occur within the classroom context. Over time, how higher education has viewed evaluation, teaching, learning, and assessment has varied dramatically.

Historical Approaches to Assessing Learning

In the nineteenth century, students had to show to the public that they had actually learned what they were supposed to have learned. "A candidate for the bachelor's, therefore, faced a final hurdle of the senior declamation . . . often these examinations were conducted orally, by and before outsiders" (Hutchings and Marchese, 1990, p. 27). As Hutchings and Marchese point out, separating teaching from the evaluation of learning was important. The results of learning were something that should be demonstrated to others. And, as a student was able to demonstrate a certain amount of learning, he (and it was typically a "he") was considered to be educated and

NEW DIRECTIONS FOR TEACHING AND LEARNING, no. 123, Fall 2010 © Wiley Periodicals, Inc.
View this article online at wileyonlinelibrary.com. • DOI: 10.1002/tl.408

was given a degree. This changed in the late 18th and early 19th centuries, as more undergraduate students came to a growing larger number of post-baccalaureate institutions. A college degree became more like what it has become today—something that was given following the fulfillment of a set of agreed-upon courses, rather than an overall knowledge of an area.

In 1935 a survey demonstrated that 252 colleges required a senior comprehensive exam (Hutchings and Marchese, 1990). But, as numbers of students and institutions continued to increase, the percentage of institutions that required a comprehensive exam decreased dramatically.

In the mid-twentieth century, it became apparent that there was a greater need to know about student learning and students, in general. A pivotal work was that of Chickering (1969), which is still cited today. Additionally, the Astin (1977) and Pascarella and Terenzini (1991) research allowed those in higher education to understand better the results of a long-term, value-added approach to studying student learning.

In the 1960s, according to Ewell (2002), program review became an important part of looking across a particular program or major. Early "program evaluation relied largely on quantitative methods" (p. 5). Because of this, surveys and cost-benefit analyses were the types of information that were collected. As the interest in quantitative data grew, many of these early program evaluations often asked how the students viewed particular programs; as a result, satisfaction surveys have continued to be a popular method to gather data. As cost-benefit analyses were often a part of program evaluation, this view of an education program being "worth" what it was costing the university became an important variable.

Also in the mid-twentieth century, the concept of mastery learning was brought back, but in a newer form called "programmed instruction," and, because of newer technology, was often able to provide students with the educational materials they needed to move at their own pace. The benefit to this type of teaching was that the student was receiving constant feedback on correct and incorrect responses. Although mastery learning has more often been used with elementary and secondary education, the concepts contained in the theory of mastery learning have been an important part of educational philosophy (Bloom, 1971). Institutions such as Evergreen State University, Alverno College, and Antioch College clearly show mastery learning as an important part of the development of "alternative" approaches for institutions (Ewell, 2002). In addition, "mastery methods posed an effective alternative to the prominent (and politically popular) "testing and measurement paradigm" that is still used today (Ewell, 2002, p. 6).

Another area that has had impact on how teaching and learning are evaluated is that of accreditation. Assessment and accreditation have grown dramatically in importance over the past several decades. And, as they have grown in importance, they have, sadly, become separated from the practice of teaching and learning. Although both accountability and enhancement of student learning are important aspects of assessment, it is crucial to come to an agreement about the core purpose of assessing learning. "Though accountability matters, learning still matters most" (Angelo, 1999, p. 3). And, if learning matters most, the evaluation of learning is an increasingly important topic. Although there may be a need to demonstrate learning to others through accreditation, the most valuable purpose in assessing learning is knowing how to improve and enhance teaching so that learning continues to grow. However, understanding the historical context of accreditation is useful in understanding how it can impact teaching and learning decisions.

Accreditation in Historical Perspective

Faculty members usually know quite clearly what their students have learned and what they have not learned. In general, many faculty use this information to make modifications to their courses and sometimes even to the overall sequencing of courses. Using data in this way has been called "transformative assessment," and is intended to enhance teaching and learning in an ongoing, meaningful, and appropriate way (Wehlburg, 2008). Unfortunately, discussions of accreditation often do not begin with the concept of learning.

Banta (2007) asked, "Can assessment for accountability and assessment for improvement coexist? Can the current accountability focus actually strengthen assessment for improvement? Or will an accountability tidal wave roll across the fields, crushing the fragile green sprouts of assessment for improvement that have begun to appear?" (p. 9). These types of questions clearly demonstrate the pressure that exists between accountability and improving teaching. Too often, faculty are caught in the middle of this debate. The overall institution needs to be held accountable to accrediting agencies, boards, parents, and others, whereas faculty members generally want to focus on teaching and learning within their courses. Because the term *assessment* has so often been linked only to accountability purposes, it is not surprising that this tension exists and that many faculty members recognize the impact that assessment can have on teaching and learning.

The first accreditation bodies were begun in the 1890s, in large part because of the rapid increase in the number and types of institutions of higher education and the public interest in "identifying institutions of trustworthy educational quality" (Brittingham, 2009, p. 13). Early on in their development, accreditation organizations focused mainly on developing specific criteria in order for institutions to become members. It wasn't until the 1950s that regional accrediting bodies began to implement the methods that are now in use, including a set of standards or principles, a self-study, and a periodic reporting system using peer evaluators. As Brittingham further points out, however, "standards have moved from quantitative to qualitative, from prescriptive to mission centered, and from minimal to aspirational" (Brittingham, 2009, p. 15). Accreditation has clearly gone beyond merely counting the books in a library and is now focused on using student learning data to develop a system of continuous enhancement of improving learning. And, although many faculty see accreditation and assessment as a barrier to focusing on teaching and learning, this accountability approach does have benefits. Without the requirement from accrediting agencies regarding the need for assessment, the assessment movement would never have grown as it has. Clearly, decisions made by regional and specialized accrediting agencies have caused institutions to look seriously at learning outcomes and to determine methods to identify and measure them in meaningful and appropriate ways, and then use the results for improvement. The top-down approach to mandating unfortunately has led, at times, to the institutional perspective that assessment is "a means to appease the accreditors, not necessarily as a way to learn about their own institutions, because the stakes have become so high" (Schilling, 2006, p. 2).

Assessment for Accountability

The concept of assessing for accountability is probably one of the reasons that assessment has not been more useful in higher education. Assessing for accountability focuses on the need to provide information to others— usually those who are external to the institution. Accreditation boards are an excellent example of how assessment for accountability is viewed (Wehlburg, 2008). With accountability, assessment is not done for the purpose of enhancing teaching and learning—instead, it is done to demonstrate compliance with a set of assigned standards. Assessment for accountability often is typically a process that has been mandated by an outside body and for which the institution must demonstrate that it has done sufficiently well. If the institution cannot demonstrate this to others, there are all kinds of negative impacts: possible probation, loss of accreditation, and public humiliation. Clearly, no institution wants this to occur.

Imagine preparing for an accreditation visit where the fear was that something negative might be found if all wasn't in order. How would the institution prepare? Most likely, everything would be shined and polished! If there was anything that could possibly show that the institution had a problem, it would be fixed quickly or even glossed over to show that it wasn't as bad as it might seem. This practice of focusing on accountability and of only showing the good and not sharing the institution's possible areas for improvement did not work to the advantage of the institution, its faculty, or its students.

Clearly, assessing only for the purpose of accountability leads to a punishment mentality. Avoiding punishment leads to a great deal of time spent on trying to make things look good rather than to actually work to make things better. Assessment this way is likely to produce circumstances where assessing student learning outcomes are collecting only the data that demonstrate that the institution is doing well. Any possible dirty laundry is ignored—and stays dirty. According to Alstete "the current political and social environment makes the topics of accountability and accreditation extremely important. Over the past two decades, state and federal governments have been emphasizing the need for some quality assurance and improvement mechanism for higher education" (Alstete, 2004, p. xi). There truly is a need for accreditation—assessment for accountability will probably always be part of higher education, because demonstrating how well an institution is doing and whether or not it is doing what it says that it will do is important, not only for accreditation, but also for the community, parents, and future students. Accountability is an important part of higher education, but it is not the only part (and it is certainly not the most important aspect of learning).

Transformative Assessment

In contrast with assessment for accountability, transformative assessment should be appropriate, meaningful, sustainable, flexible, and ongoing, and should use data for improvement with the potential for substantive change. In addition to this, the transformative assessment process must exist within a culture that expects the results to be important and useful. Angelo (1999) has outlined four pillars of transformative assessment.

The first is to build shared trust. "The point is not to start with problems and debate, but by helping participants feel respected, valued, safe, and in the company of worthy peers" (Angelo, 1999, p. 5). Faculty must feel that information learned through the assessment process will be used in ways that have been agreed upon. The success of this process is dependent on finding out what is not working as well. Only then can those areas in need of enhancement be identified. The administration, for their part, must trust that the faculty will participate fully in the process of identifying outcomes, measurements, and in the analysis and use of the findings.

Secondly, according to Angelo, it is essential to build shared motivation. "Collectively identify goals worth working toward and problems worth solving—and consider the likely costs and benefits" (Angelo, 1999, p. 5). Most members of the department, program, or even institution need to agree with the overall goals and outcomes identified for assessment. The third of Angelo's pillars is to build a shared language. "Building a shared vision for transformative change requires shared mental models and shared language for describing and manipulating those models" (Angelo, 1999, p. 6). For example, if one of the outcomes that will be developed focuses on global awareness, it is essential that all involved understand what is being meant by that term. It doesn't necessarily matter what the agreed-upon definitions are, just that everyone involved understands what they mean.

NEW DIRECTIONS FOR TEACHING AND LEARNING • DOI: 10.1002/tl

And finally, build shared guidelines (Angelo, 1999). What are the principles that are important? How will members of the institution know that things are improving? A process of transformative assessment will give higher education the information that it needs to decide upon the areas that can and should be changed. There are challenges to overcome, certainly, but by learning from history, innovative and meaningful change will take place.

Higher education has looked at learning in a variety of ways. The political and social context has and will continue to shape how learning is measured. But the one constant throughout the history of evaluating teaching is that teaching leads to learning. Learning must continue to be at the core of what higher education does. No matter what the state or national mandates require, teaching and learning is education.

References

Alstete, J. Accreditation Matters: Achieving Academic Reorganization and Renewal. Association for the Study of Higher Education—ASHE-ERIC Higher Education Report, Vol. 30, No. 4. San Francisco: Jossey-Bass, 2004.

Angelo, T. "Doing Assessment as if Learning Matters Most." AAHE Bulletin, 1999, 51(9), 3–6.

Astin, A. Four Critical Years. San Francisco: Jossey-Bass, 1977.

Banta, T. "If we must compare...." Assessment Update, 2007, 19(2), 3–4.

Bloom, B. Mastery Learning. New York: Holt, Rinehart, & Winston, 1971.

Brittingham, B. "Accreditation in the United States: How Did We Get to Where We Are?" New Directions for Higher Education, 2009, 145, 7–27.

Chickering, A. W. Education and Identity. San Francisco: Jossey-Bass, 1969.

Ewell, P. Perpetual Movement: Assessment After Twenty Years. Boulder, Colo.: National Center for Higher Education Management Systems. [http://www.teaglefoundation.org/learning/pdf/2002_ewell.pdf]. 2002.

Hutchings, P., and Marchese, T. "Watching Assessment: Questions, Stories, Prospects." Change, 1990, 22, 12–38.

Pascarella, E., and Terenzini, P. How College Affects Students: Findings and Insights from Twenty Years of Research. San Francisco: Jossey-Bass, 1991.

Schilling, K. "Assessment Methods Should Match Institutional Goals." Academic Leader, 2006, 22, 2(6).

Wehlburg, C. Promoting Integrated and Transformative Assessment: A Deeper Focus on Student Learning. San Francisco: Jossey-Bass, 2008.

CATHERINE M. WEHLBURG is the assistant provost for Institutional Effectiveness at Texas Christian University. She has taught psychology and educational psychology courses for more than a decade, serving as department chair for some of that time and then branching out into faculty development and assessment. Dr. Wehlburg has worked with both the Higher Learning Commission of the North Central Association and the Commission on Colleges with the Southern Association of Colleges and Schools as an outside evaluator.

6

Since the 1980s, advocates for change in higher education have called for double-loop learning. One of the main criticisms of the evaluation of colleges and universities was that they measured inputs rather than the outputs. Higher education now needs to apply the lessons of learning and change to campus leadership and organization.

The Learning-Paradigm Campus: From Single- to Double-Loop Learning

John Tagg

Colleges and universities have changed dramatically in the past fifty years—roughly since the end of the Second World War. But at first, they changed by growing. Between 1950 and 1970 college enrollment tripled. Many new colleges and universities were established during this period, and existing ones grew rapidly. In these decades change largely meant extending existing programs and services to more students.

Over the past thirty years thoughtful analysts of higher education have increasingly called for transformation rather than accretion, for fundamental change in the way colleges and universities are constituted, rather than just adjustment of conventional practices. A notable milestone in this shift of emphasis was the 1983 publication of *A Nation at Risk*, the report of the National Commission on Excellence in Education (1983), with its now-familiar warning that "the educational foundations of our society are presently being eroded by a rising tide of mediocrity that threatens our very future as a nation and a people." Although more often associated with K–12 education, the commission's report to the Secretary of Education consistently addressed the challenges faced by "schools and colleges."

In 1984, the Study Group on the Conditions of Excellence in American Higher Education released its report *Involvement in Learning: Reclaiming the Potential of American Higher Education*. Building on a substantial body of research by Alexander Astin and others, the report challenged the conventional practice of evaluating colleges and universities on the basis of their inputs: "endowments' and expenditures, the breadth and depth of

NEW DIRECTIONS FOR TEACHING AND LEARNING, no. 123, Fall 2010 © Wiley Periodicals, Inc.
View this article online at wileyonlinelibrary.com. • DOI: 10.1002/tl.409

curricular offerings, the intellectual attainments of faculty, the test scores of entering students." The problem with these "proxies for educational excellence" was that "none of them tells us what students actually learn and how much they grow as a result of higher education. As a result, we have no way of knowing how academic institutions actually perform" (Study Group on the Conditions of Excellence in American Higher Education, 1984, p. 15).

The Association of American Colleges (now the Association of American Colleges and Universities) followed in 1985 with *Integrity in the College Curriculum: A Report to the Academic Community*, which lamented "the loss of integrity in the bachelor's degree" (Association of American Colleges, 1985). Ten years after *A Nation at Risk*, the Wingspread Group on Higher Education, chaired by former Labor Secretary William Brock, declared that "The American imperative for the 21st century is that society must hold higher education to much higher expectations or risk national decline" (Wingspread Group on Higher Education, 1993, p. 16).

The calls for reform that began in the 1980s were challenging colleges and universities not to do more of the same, but to do something different. The demand was for a qualitative change, not just a quantitative one. It was for second-order rather than first-order change, for double-loop rather than single-loop learning, for a paradigm shift (Barr and Tagg, 1995; Tagg, 2003).

Espoused Theories and Theories-in-Use

Argyris and Schön (1974, 1996) have pointed out that organizations hold and represent knowledge, and that they thereby facilitate *theories of action*. But theories of action come in two types. When we ask individuals how people ought to behave in a given situation, the answers they would give to such a question reflect their *espoused theory*. Espoused theories are the consciously held beliefs that people express to explain, justify, or predict actions. However, if we observe people doing what they do in the organization and extract from that observation the rules that they are following, what we find is that people's behavior often does not follow their espoused theories. People don't always do what they say they should do. But the way people actually behave is not random; it follows a consistent pattern. People's behavior is generally governed by a coherent set of rules with explanatory and predictive value, a *theory-in-use*. Espoused theories are the ideas that people consciously accept and usually do believe in. But usually they do not govern our behavior. Theories-in-use do govern behavior, but we are usually unaware of them; they are held unconsciously. As Argyris puts it, "Although people [often] do not behave congruently with their espoused theories…they do behave congruently with their theories-in-use, *and* they are unaware of this fact" (Argyris, 1982, p. 85).

Speaking of the organizations we call colleges and universities, Astin observed, "Institutions espouse high-sounding values, of course, in their mission statements, college catalogues, and public pronouncements by institutional leaders. The problem is that the explicitly stated values— which always include a strong commitment to undergraduate education— are often at variance with the actual values that drive our decisions and policies" (Astin, 1993, p. 235). In other words, the espoused theories of higher education organizations and those who run them are often inconsistent with their theories-in-use.

Single-Loop and Double-Loop Learning

When we act for a purpose, we receive feedback from the environment that tells us whether the purpose has been achieved. Normally, we learn to adjust our action strategies directly in response to feedback. This is called "single-loop learning." Argyris and Schön (1974), following cybernetics theorist Ross Ashby, used the simple example of a thermostat to illustrate this process. The governing value in this system is the thermostat setting, say 76°. The feedback loop is from consequences to action strategy. It might be diagrammed this way:

Usually, single-loop learning will suffice. But if circumstances change and new factors are introduced, it might not. What, for example, if the humidity changes, so that what was a comfortable temperature yesterday becomes unpleasant?

If we are going to achieve the desired consequences, we now need to change not just the action strategies, but also the governing values behind them. When the single-loop approach fails to achieve the consequence of a comfortable environment, the only way to get better results is to move up to *double-loop learning*. In the case of the heating/cooling system, when 76° proves too warm for a muggy day with a room full of people, we need to adjust the governing value to 72°.

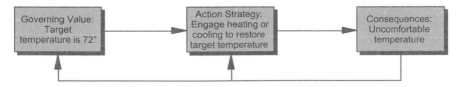

Single-loop learning leads to first-order change and innovation. Double-loop learning leads to second-order change and transformation. At the highest level of generalization, double-loop learning leads to a paradigm shift, to a change in the fundamental governing values that define the institution (Barr and Tagg, 1995; Tagg, 2003, 2007).

For an example of how this concept might apply in colleges and universities, consider the academic core of most institutions: the curriculum. The theory-in-use of most colleges is built on the assumption that the curriculum is conveyed through a series of classes, and that what the teachers of those classes "cover" defines the curriculum. The action strategies that these governing values authorize are all contained in separate classes, are at the discretion of individual teachers, and look something like this:

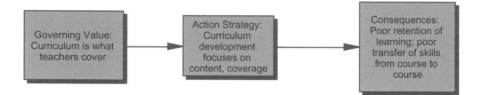

When things go wrong, and the consequences are not satisfactory, the single-loop response to the problems is to alter course by altering the courses:

It is certainly not the case that the curriculum doesn't change. Indeed, changing the curriculum, defined as the list of courses taught or the content of those courses, is a subject of frequent, sometimes intense, controversy on many campuses. What is not clear is that the changes that result make much difference. Astin found in his longitudinal studies of the effects of different general education curricula that "what specific options are offered, how much freedom of choice is allowed, and whether particular types of courses are required do not appear to have any substantial effect on how students develop during their undergraduate years" (Astin, 1993, p. 425). So the single-loop response of curricular change by content management, while it may have a Hawthorne effect for a short time, hardly ever makes a dent in the underlying academic problems. What Astin found is that "how students *approach* general education (and how the faculty actually *deliver* the curriculum) is far more important than the formal curricular content and structure" (Astin, 1993, p. 425). But this insight moves us toward double-loop learning; it suggests that we have to rethink what curriculum is, how it works, and what it's for. If we make the second learning loop, we try on a new value: curriculum isn't what teachers teach; it's what students learn.

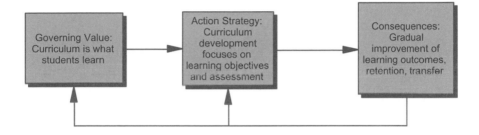

In the conventional institution, the list of classes is the solid basis for our thinking, and the content in the syllabus is what we can manipulate to try to get better results. Learning outcomes, on the other hand, are a kind of window dressing, something we are required to do for bureaucratic reasons, but we can dispense with them without touching our sense of the core, essential operations of the college. If we change the governing value, then learning outcomes, descriptions of what students learn, become the real curriculum, the solid reality that is the framework of our thinking, and classes are just one possible means to the end. Then, what shows up in the student's portfolio is much more salient than what shows up on the professor's syllabus. And what the syllabus says about how students will learn is as important as the descriptions of what they will learn.

Since the 1980s, advocates for change in higher education have conspicuously called for double-loop learning, and of a specific kind. *A Nation at Risk* struck the theme with its call for "a learning society." The core criticism that the Study Group made in 1984 was that colleges and universities measured inputs rather than the outputs. The report called unambiguously and clearly for a shift of emphasis from inputs and processes to one on outcomes, specifically the learning outcomes experienced by students. In 1995, Robert Barr and I formulated this issue specifically as a challenge to the established theory-in-use of most institutions of higher education, which was aimed at offering classes and maintaining enrollment: "the paradigm that has governed our colleges is this: A college is an institution that exists *to provide instruction.* Subtly but profoundly we are shifting to a new paradigm: A college is an institution that exists *to produce learning*" (Barr and Tagg, 1995, p. 25). The learning paradigm is very close to the espoused

NEW DIRECTIONS FOR TEACHING AND LEARNING • DOI: 10.1002/tl

theories of most educators—we see it reflected in presidential addresses and college catalogues. But the instruction paradigm is much closer to the theory-in-use of most colleges. Edgerton, president emeritus of the AAHE, assumed the leadership of higher education programs for the Pew Charitable Trusts in 1997, declaring his priorities in an influential white paper. "The key," he wrote, "is to think first in terms of student learning, and then reengineer the way academic work gets done from this perspective" (Edgerton, 1997).

Innovation or Transformation?

The last three decades have seen large-scale innovation in colleges and universities. In 1985 the American Association for Higher Education (AAHE) held its first Assessment Conference, and Campus Compact was established. In 1986 the National Center for the Study of the Freshman Year Experience was founded, and in 1987 the Washington Center for Improving the Quality of Undergraduate Education was founded. In 1990 Boyer, then president of the Carnegie Foundation for the Advancement of Teaching, introduced the idea of the scholarship of teaching and learning in his book *Scholarship Reconsidered* (Boyer, 1990). Lee Shulman became president of the Carnegie Foundation in 1997, created the Carnegie Academy for the Scholarship of Teaching and Learning (CASTL), and initiated extensive studies of pedagogy in various fields. In 1997, Edgerton moved to Pew and advanced dozens of innovative programs, the most consequential of which has probably been the National Survey of Student Engagement (NSSE), which began in 1998. The Association of American Colleges and Universities, under the leadership of Carol Geary Schneider, undertook the work of defining liberal education and promoting learning outcomes and meaningful assessment, especially with its Greater Expectations report (Association of American Colleges and Universities, 2005). These and other organizations, many with governmental or foundation support, sought to promote innovations of various kinds, and most have been notably successful in doing so. Many of these programs have been initiated with truly transformative intent. But how, and how deeply, have they changed adopting institutions?

Is this happening? The closing decades of the twentieth century were seen by many at the time as "the Golden Age of Innovation." But it is fair to ask whether the innovations were first-order or second-order change, whether institutions were involved in single-loop or double-loop learning. As the century drew to a close, many analysts concluded that what we saw in the Golden Age was more gilding than gold. For example, Lazerson, Wagener, and Shumanis of the Institution for Research on Higher Education at the University of Pennsylvania concluded that "While the repertoire of innovative teaching practices grows, we are uncertain that institutional leaders are connecting incremental changes to *systemic* strategies for making teaching and learning a central, highly rewarded activity on their campuses" (Lazerson, Wagener, and Shumanis, 2000, p. 19). O'Banion, president of the league for Innovation in the Community College, began his book *A Learning College for the 21st Century* with a review of reform efforts, and found that "The primary problem of education reform triggered by *A Nation at Risk* is that solutions have been proposed as add-ons or modifications to the current system of education. Tweaking the current system by adding on the *innovation du jour* will not be sufficient." Indeed, he compared the previous decade of innovation to "trimming the branches of a dying tree" (O'Banion, 1997, p. 7).

Assessment: The Lever

There are, of course, many barriers, beginning with organizational structure, that impede double-loop learning (Tagg, 2008). But what keeps institutions locked in single-loop learning more than anything else is the dearth of information on most campuses about either teaching or learning. The feedback loops that cause organizational learning consist of information about what has happened as a result of the action strategies we have adopted. Today, most institutions have extensive information about the movement of students through the institution. Department chairs, deans, provosts, and presidents can tell us how many students are enrolled in courses and programs, what grades they have received, how far they have advanced toward a degree, and what the graduation rates are. In other words, institutions know how many students and which students have received instruction, and how quickly they are advancing through the instructional pipeline. But at most institutions, no one can tell us whether those same students have worked collaboratively with other students, what kinds of assignments they have done, what kind of tests they have taken, how many books they have read, and what they have learned in the course of their studies. It is not that administrators are negligent in not having this information; the information simply doesn't exist. Many institutions have expressed the intention, in vision or mission statements or strategic plans, to change the governing values that guide their decision making, to become more learning-centered or learner-centered. They face a daunting challenge, however, if they have no direct data on what and how students are learning.

Thus, assessment of student learning is the lever that, with the fulcrum of student learning outcomes, can move institutions to transformative rather than cosmetic change. Solid evidence of what, how much, and where students are learning can directly challenge the governing values of the existing paradigm and facilitate double-loop learning. But the movement to make meaningful learning assessment standard practice has faced daunting challenges. The good news is that that movement has gained momentum over the years. The disappointing news is that institutions have moved to define and assess student learning outcomes with a spirit of lugubrious vacillation that makes procrastinating undergraduates appear sprightly and engaged by comparison.

The Tension Between Accountability and Improvement

One source of confusion is the purpose of assessing learning outcomes. Alongside the developing argument for reform inside of higher education, outside entities—the federal government, the states, and the accrediting bodies—have increasingly called for evidence of performance. External demands for accountability and internal pressures for reform often emerge as responses to the same evidence. Ewell, Vice President of the National Center for Higher Education Management Systems (NCHEMS) and Senior Scholar at the new National Institute for Learning Outcomes Assessment (NILOA), has been an advocate for and close observer of assessment work throughout the whole period in question. At the end of 2009, he reflected on a paper he presented to the AAHE's Third National Assessment Forum in 1987. In many ways, the issues were strikingly similar. Today, as twenty years ago, Ewell notes a "conceptual tension" between two views—what today he calls "two paradigms of assessment": assessment for improvement and assessment for accountability. The "external" agencies to which colleges and universities are chiefly accountable have changed. In the 1980s they were state governments; today the regional accreditation agencies take point. The federal government, mainly through the extended deliberations and final report of the Spellings Commission, has created an aura of accountability, even in the absence of distinct policy changes. But just as extrinsic rewards and punishments tend to depress intrinsic motivation in students, the prospect of external accountability has often displaced, rather than reinforced, institutional improvement as a purpose for learning assessment. Ewell writes, "Far too many institutions, dominated by the need to respond to external actors like states or accreditors, approach the task of assessment as an act of compliance, with the objective being simply to measure something and the exercise ending as soon as the data are reported" (Ewell, 2009, p. 16).

That accountability has become, for some at least, the enemy of improvement is dramatic testimony to the perverse workings of the law of unintended consequences, for certainly that outcome could please no one. But it remains true that the process of assessment for improvement can, if properly structured, satisfy the call for accountability.

Better Tools, Clearer Tasks

Although the majority of institutions have not engaged in double-loop learning, some have—and much else has changed. Ongoing research on the way the mind works and the way people learn has made the traditional arguments from ignorance ("Well, we just don't know . . ."; "There hasn't been enough research . . .") less persuasive. Resistance to assessment and learning outcomes, while still with us, seems to be fading. Ewell notes that, "Although assessment probably remains distasteful to many faculty members, it is angrily rejected far less frequently than it was 20 years ago" (Ewell, 2009, p. 6). The steps that institutions need to take to produce significant improvements in student learning are much more clearly defined than they have ever been.

Furthermore, the tools are now available to do what needs to be done. Pioneering colleges like Alverno, Olivet, and Kings have demonstrated that comprehensive assessment and systematic feedback to students and faculty framed by clearly defined learning outcomes is possible. Technological support systems such as eLumen have greatly simplified the development and use of learning outcomes and rubrics and allow institutions to aggregate the evidence of student performance so that it can serve as feedback to students, faculty, and the institution. Digital portfolios allow institutions to preserve the products of student learning, and if linked to a systematic set of learning outcomes such portfolios and outcome "transcripts," can provide an alternative to the lists of courses that pass for a curriculum at most institutions. The pedagogical approaches that produce learning are increasingly clear, and the evidence for them is increasingly strong. As Pascarella and Terenzini conclude in the second volume of their massive meta-analysis of research on higher education, "With striking consistency, studies show that innovative, active collaborative, cooperative, and constructivist instructional approaches shape learning more powerfully, in some forms by substantial margins, than do conventional lecture-discussion and text-based approaches" (Pascarella and Terenzini, 2005, p. 646). And the growing acceptance of the scholarship of teaching and learning means that the evidence will mount even more rapidly in the future to define what works for learning.

A Teachable Moment

What has happened over the past thirty years is that the groundwork has been laid for mission-directed organizational learning. The pieces are all in place. It is a teachable moment for colleges and universities. Furthermore, tools like the National Survey of Student Engagement (NSSE) and the Collegiate Learning Assessment (CLA) are providing a growing body of information about what is going on at college campuses and how well it is working. There are two problems with tools like the NSSE and the CLA. First, they are private. In many cases the results are not publicly available, and sometimes not even to the faculty and staff of the institution. Second, they provide global rather than local information—information about the whole institution, not localized to specific divisions of the institution, colleges, departments, teachers, or students. Thus the information produced, while valuable, is not directly actionable.

NEW DIRECTIONS FOR TEACHING AND LEARNING • DOI: 10.1002/tl

What this new information does is undermine confidence in the governing values that have long been assumed at many institutions. It provides good evidence that the system is not working as well as it could, that it needs attention and correction. At the same time, the evidence of cognitive science and psychology has become widely available, in ways that teachers can implement at the classroom level the work of many fine scholar-practitioners, including Weimer (2002), Fink (2003), Svinicki (2004), and Doyle (2008).

Double-loop learning at the institutional level cannot take place in the classroom. Harris and Cullen, in their new book *Leading the Learner Centered Campus* (Harris and Cullen, 2010), point out quite correctly that "if the comprehensive shift to a new paradigm is to become a reality, then the efforts to transform our practices need to extend beyond the classroom." Indeed, we need to apply the lessons of learning and change to campus leadership and organization. In important ways, organizations learn the same way individuals do. The first prerequisite for both is a learning environment in which they can receive meaningful feedback on the consequences of their actions. Today, we know what information is important, and we know how to collect it and feed it back to those who need it. All the elements are in place to test the hypothesis that institutions of higher learning can, in fact, learn.

References

Argyris, C. *Reasoning, Learning, and Action: Individual and Organizational*. San Francisco: Jossey-Bass, 1982.

Argyris, C., and Schön, D. A. *Theory in Practice*. San Francisco: Jossey-Bass, 1974.

Argyris, C., and Schön, D. A. *Organizational Learning II: Theory, Method and Practice*. Reading, Mass.: Addison-Wesley, 1996.

Association of American Colleges. *Integrity in the College Curriculum: A Report to the Academic Community*. Washington, D.C.: Association of American Colleges, 1985.

Association of American Colleges and Universities. *Greater Expectations: A New Vision for Learning as a Nation Goes to College*. Washington, D.C.: Association of American Colleges and Universities, 2005.

Astin, A. W. *What Matters in College? Four Critical Years Revisited*. San Francisco: Jossey-Bass, 1993.

Barr, R. B., and Tagg, J. "From Teaching to Learning: A New Paradigm for Undergraduate Education." *Change*, 1995, 27(6), 12–25.

Boyer, E. *Scholarship Reconsidered: Priorities of the Professoriate*. Princeton, N.J.: The Carnegie Foundation for the Advancement of Teaching, 1990.

Doyle, T. *Helping Students Learn in a Learner-Centered Environment: A Guide to Facilitating Learning in Higher Education*. Sterling, Va.: Stylus, 2008.

Edgerton, R. *Education White Paper*. Washington, D.C.: Pew Charitable Trusts, 1997.

Ewell, P. T. *Assessment, Accountability, and Improvement: Revisiting the Tension*. Washington, D.C.: National Institute for Learning Outcomes Assessment, 2009. http://learningoutcomesassessment.org/documents/PeterEwell.pdf.

Fink, L. D. *Creating Significant Learning Experiences: An Integrated Approach to Designing College Courses*. San Francisco: Jossey-Bass, 2003.

NEW DIRECTIONS FOR TEACHING AND LEARNING • DOI: 10.1002/tl

Harris, M., and Cullen, R. *Leading the Learner-Centered Campus: An Administrator's Framework for Improving Student Learning Outcomes.* San Francisco: Jossey-Bass, 2010.

Lazerson, M., Wagener, U., and Shumanis, N. "Teaching and Learning in Higher Education, 1980–2000." *Change 32(3)*, 2000, 12–19.

National Commission on Excellence in Education. *A Nation at Risk: The Imperative for Educational Reform.* Washington, D.C.: National Commission on Excellence in Education, 1983. http://www.ed.gov/pubs/NatAtRisk/index.html.

O'Banion, T. A. *Learning College for the 21st Century.* Phoenix: Oryx Press, 1997.

Pascarella, E. T., and Terenzini, P. T. *How College Affects Students: Volume 2: A Third Decade of Research.* San Francisco: Jossey-Bass, 2005.

Study Group on the Conditions of Excellence in American Higher Education. *Involvement in Learning: Realizing the Potential of American Higher Education.* Washington, D.C.: National Institute of Education, 1984. (ED 246 833)

Svinicki, M. D. *Learning and Motivation in the Postsecondary Classroom.* Bolton, Mass.: Anker, 2004.

Tagg, J. *The Learning Paradigm College.* Bolton, Mass.: Anker, 2003.

Tagg, J. "Double-Loop Learning in Higher Education." *Change*, 2007, 39(4), 36–41.

Tagg, J. "Changing Minds in Higher Education: Students Change, So Why Can't Colleges?" *Planning for Higher Education*, 37(1), 2008, 15–22.

Weimer, M. *Learner-Centered Teaching: Five Key Changes to Practice.* San Francisco: Jossey-Bass, 2002.

Wingspread Group on Higher Education. *An American Imperative: Higher Expectations for Higher Education.* Racine, Wis.: The Johnson Foundation, 1993.

JOHN TAGG is an independent writer and consultant and an advocate for organizational change in higher education to better advance student learning. He is author of The Learning Paradigm College *(Jossey-Bass, 2003) and professor emeritus of English at Palomar College, where he taught from 1982 to 2009. He has published work on higher education reform in* Change, About Campus, On the Horizon, Planning for Higher Education, *and other publications. He serves on the Editorial Review Board of the* International Journal for the Scholarship of Teaching and Learning *and the* Journal on Centers for Teaching and Learning.

7

The scholarship of teaching and learning is one development that has occurred over the last twenty-five years. This chapter argues that it is best understood as a habit of mind and set of practices that contribute to a culture in which other changes and developments can thrive.

The Scholarship of Teaching and Learning: From Idea to Integration

Pat Hutchings

Metaphors about graveyards and slow-moving ships have long been commonplace in descriptions of higher education and its pace of change. But as this volume attests, the reality is more complicated. By way of example, I think of my own experience as an undergraduate in the early 1970s. I was one of those students who leapt into college life with both feet and loved (just about) every minute of it. But looking back, I am struck not only by what those years included, but also by what they didn't. There were no small-group collaborative learning experiences, no learning communities, no service-learning, no undergraduate research offerings, no electronic portfolios, no problem-based learning—indeed, very few of the practices that are now seen as hallmarks of a powerful learning environment. Granted, such opportunities are still far from universally available. And the embrace of them in even the most reform-minded, learning-focused settings may still be fragile. But clearly it is not the case that there is nothing new under the higher education sun. This essay, then, looks at the scholarship of teaching and learning as one development among many over the last twenty-five years, arguing that it is best understood not as a discrete new model or approach but as a habit of mind and set of practices that contribute to a culture in which other changes and developments can thrive. By engaging faculty from a wide range of fields in asking and answering questions about their students' learning, the scholarship of teaching and learning inspires, shapes, and informs further advances in teaching, curriculum, assessment, and campus culture.

NEW DIRECTIONS FOR TEACHING AND LEARNING, no. 123, Fall 2010 © Wiley Periodicals, Inc.
View this article online at wileyonlinelibrary.com. • DOI: 10.1002/tl.410

Coming to Terms

The language of the scholarship of teaching and learning first gained prominence in higher education through the volume by Carnegie Foundation president Ernest Boyer, *Scholarship Reconsidered: Priorities of the Professoriate* (Boyer, 1990). But the idea captured in the phrase has a longer and more varied lineage, drawing on earlier work on teacher knowledge (Shulman, 1987), more traditional educational research coming out of schools of education, the study of learning and cognition (McKeachie, 1980), the teacher research movement in K–12 settings (Cochran-Smith and Lytle, 1999), and the student assessment movement—especially the practices of classroom assessment and classroom research (Angelo and Cross, 1993). The work has been fed by fields (like chemistry and composition) that have a notable history of pedagogical research as well, and by the proliferation of campus teaching centers, which have provided a foundation for such work by bringing faculty together to look carefully at their teaching and their students' work. Additionally, and in a more general way, the scholarship of teaching and learning has been shaped by the rise of action research and the recognition of the value of practitioner knowledge (Schön, 1983; Shulman, 1987, 2004).

Given the diverse genetic pool contributing to the scholarship of teaching and learning, it is no surprise that Boyer's phrase was understood in different ways. (Boyer did not, in fact, include "learning," in the original formulation; it was added in Carnegie's subsequent work and has now become common usage.) The 1990s were marked by lively debates about what this new concept did and did not include, about definitions and boundaries. How was the scholarship of teaching and learning related to good teaching? If it was more than teaching excellence, what were the added elements? What forms might it take? Was it something any faculty member might do, or a type of work that demanded special skills and background and was thus only for a small group of specialists? How could its quality be measured, and how would it be valued and rewarded? These and other questions were front and center as campuses looked for ways to engage with the idea and hammered their way toward locally meaningful conceptions of the work it implied. On research universities, for instance, the scholarship of teaching and learning was typically understood in ways that parallel traditional research—as peer-reviewed, published scholarship, that is. In settings more narrowly focused on teaching, the emphasis was often on enriching local conversations about teaching and shaping innovations that improved students' learning (see Cambridge, 2004). An awareness of disciplinary differences began to emerge early on, as well (Healey, 2002; Huber and Morreale, 2002).

This line of conceptual debate and deliberation continues today and has resulted in a rich literature about the defining features of the scholarship of teaching and learning (Bass, 1999; Kreber, 2001), its difference from related (and equally important) kinds of pedagogical work (Hutchings and Shulman, 1999; Trigwell, 2004), its methods (McKinney, 2007), and its underlying conceptual and theoretical bases (Hutchings and Huber, 2008; Roxä, Olsson, and Märtensson, 2008). For some, perhaps, the continuing attention to "what it is" may seem to lean toward navel-gazing. But definitions matter, sending powerful signals about who is welcome in such work, who is excluded, and about purposes and values. In general the debates have been healthy, keeping the field open and emergent, and making it a welcoming place for educators from many different contexts, with opportunities for cross fertilization and solid connections to the wider "teaching commons" (Huber and Hutchings, 2005) in which communities of educators committed to pedagogical inquiry and innovation come together to exchange ideas.

From Idea to Action

Over the past dozen years, I have had a special perch for watching the scholarship of teaching and learning movement unfold. As a senior scholar and vice president at The Carnegie Foundation for the Advancement of Teaching, I was part of a team that led and learned from the Carnegie Academy for the Scholarship of Teaching and Learning (CASTL), an ambitious effort, running from 1998–2009, to propel this new idea and language into action: in the practice of individual faculty members; as a conception of faculty work in a wide range of disciplines and professional fields; and as an aspect of campus life and work. These three arenas offer a useful framework for tracing how this idea has taken shape, what has happened, and where things are headed. (Readers looking for a fuller account of the CASTL program should consult Cambridge, 2004; Ciccone, 2009; Gale, 2007; Huber, 2010.)

Individual Teaching Practice. One measure of the trajectory of the scholarship of teaching and learning has been its capacity to engage growing numbers of faculty from a broad range of settings. What was once an intriguing if sometimes puzzling idea—of interest to a small group of faculty—has over the past decade catalyzed a sizable and significant international community of scholars. Although exact numbers are impossible to know, one indicator of this broad engagement is the International Society for the Scholarship of Teaching and Learning. Established in 2004, the organization's 2009 annual meeting (the sixth) drew some 650 participants, from 500 institutions, and 15 countries (see www.issotl.org). The variety of their work is telling, as well, ranging widely across disciplines and fields, employing a full array of methods from individual case studies to larger-scale surveys, and exploring questions about particular classroom innovations on the one hand and more broad-based theories of learning and expertise on the other.

NEW DIRECTIONS FOR TEACHING AND LEARNING • DOI: 10.1002/tl

The pathways by which these scholars enter this community are varied. Some become involved through a campus initiative that raises questions about the efficacy of a new approach. Others enter through a disciplinary or departmental door, engaging with new ideas about the field and what it means to bring novice learners to advanced levels of understanding and practice. Although the initial impulse is typically local, involvement with national projects often prompts questions that invite the scholarship of teaching and learning. And in some settings, the call for program or institutional assessment has usefully intersected with the kinds of inquiry faculty can conduct in their own classrooms. As in most engaging work, a sense of common cause and colleagueship adds fuel to the fire. For many faculty, the chance to share their findings with others—in writing, public presentations, and also, increasingly, in new multimedia, Web-based formats—encourages larger ambitions and deeper engagement.

What is also clear is that such work can be personally transformative, even "disruptive," as suggested by a comment from a young faculty member in history who became involved in the scholarship of teaching and learning: "As a new professor, drunk on the high spirits distilled from positive course evaluations, I rested easily in the knowledge . . . that I was a 'great,' 'superb,' 'wonderful' teacher," he noted. "But I'm younger than that now." He goes on to talk about his effort to design his teaching more carefully and his choice to "live discerningly with the scholarship of teaching and learning" rather than "happily without it, but deceived" (quoted in Huber and Hutchings, 2005, p. 73). Although not all scholars of teaching and learning confess to such mind-changing experiences, treating one's classroom as a site for inquiry is eye-opening and career-altering for many. Ninety-eight percent of faculty who served as CASTL Scholars (a nationally selective fellowship program) reported that the work increased their excitement about teaching; ninety-three percent changed the design of their courses; ninety-two percent found that their expectations about their own students' learning were changed (Huber and Hutchings, 2005, p. 140).

Developments in the Scholarly and Professional Societies. Scholars of teaching and learning are powerful recruiters of new talent as they share their work in informal conversations on campus, at more formal campus events featuring local scholarship of teaching and learning, in presentations and workshops at national and international conferences, and on the Web. But in addition to this grassroots dynamic, such work has spread and evolved as a result of leadership within the disciplinary communities that shape faculty identity and send powerful signals about what does and does not constitute serious scholarly work.

Such leadership was cultivated early on when representatives of a range of scholarly and professional societies were brought together to explore emerging conceptions of scholarly work. The immediate impetus was *Scholarship Reconsidered*, but interest was catalyzed as well by the more general concern that higher education was seen as neglectful of teaching (and other more applied, integrative aspects of faculty work). In response, many of these groups issued statements advocating openness to a wider range of scholarship and affirming the importance of teaching as consequential, intellectual work (Diamond and Adam, 1995). Though not all of the groups invoked the language of the scholarship of teaching and learning, the general spirit of the idea was clearly in evidence.

Over the following decade (sometimes but not always in conjunction with CASTL, which convened scholarly and professional societies and offered seed grants to support their work), many of these groups turned their resolutions into action, for instance by creating new journals dedicated to the scholarship of teaching and learning in their field, or by making a place for such work in existing, high-visibility journals, as was true in history (see Pace, 2004). Other groups established new conferences and venues, bringing scholars of teaching and learning together. Some created training programs and pursued new funding sources. The National Academy of Engineering called for work on engineering education to be recognized as research, and created the Center for the Advancement of Scholarship on Engineering Education, and the Howard Hughes Medical Institute gave out $1 million grants to 20 Howard Hughes Medical Institute fellows for scholarly projects on teaching and learning. The American Society for Microbiology has used National Science Foundation money to train some 90 biologists in the scholarship of teaching and learning, and is moving to increase that number (Chang, e-mail to Hutchings, January 4, 2010).

As these examples suggest, the scholarship of teaching and learning has taken different forms in different fields, with each bringing its own traditions, values, and resources to bear (Huber and Morreale, 2002). Along the way, they are learning from one another, borrowing ideas, and working to advance the larger cause of teaching.

Campus Culture. Throughout the development of the scholarship of teaching and learning movement, and woven through debates about definitions, methods, forms, and formats, questions about the value and status of this work on campus have been a running subtext. And this is no surprise. Such work goes against the grain in many academic settings—and not only in those heavily tilted toward traditional research. Community college faculty have, for instance, had to sort out the place of such scholarship, as well (Tinberg, Duffy, and Mino, 2007).

Certainly there are signs of progress. For starters, it is worth pointing out that more than 250 campuses signed on to participate in CASTL over its decade-plus of activity: grappling with definitions, analyzing the campus context for serious work on teaching and learning, and undertaking action initiatives of their own design to bring the scholarship of teaching and learning more fully into the institutional mainstream. The program offered $5,000 grants to a small number of campuses to support this work in the early years, but institutions were required to commit significant resources of their own as an indication of local commitment.

NEW DIRECTIONS FOR TEACHING AND LEARNING • DOI: 10.1002/tl

As might be expected, their efforts "took" more firmly in some places than others, but data on campus developments are promising. As of 2002, for instance, seventy percent of institutions reporting their work to Carnegie were providing stipends, grants, or released time for individual faculty or departments doing the scholarship of teaching and learning; ninety-five percent had sponsored campus-wide and departmental conferences, workshops, and retreats; and seventy-one percent reported developing new infrastructure (like a teaching center) to support and facilitate the work, with many pointing to its impact on professional development, where the focus on asking and answering questions about students' learning was seen by one participant as a new "lingua franca" (Ciccone, 2004, p. 49).

Over the years, policies explicitly identifying the scholarship of teaching and learning as work that counts for promotion and tenure have also been put in place (see, for example, O'Meara and Rice, 2005; Post, 2004; Roen, 2004). And although such policies do not tell the whole story—whether the work will really count depends on many factors much closer to the ground, including the scholar's ability to make a strong case to colleagues—the stage has been set for further progress with a menu of strategies for the peer review of teaching (Hutchings, 1996); extensive experience with new tools (most notably course portfolios) for documenting the scholarly work of teaching and learning (Bernstein, Burnett, Goodburn, and Savory, 2006); and case studies of individuals who have found a place for the scholarship of teaching and learning in their careers (Huber, 2004).

It should be said, as well, that promotion and tenure are not the only significant indicators of a campus's embrace of this work. As the following comment suggests, more subtle shifts in culture, leadership, and language can also be important:

> Our experience [with the scholarship of teaching and learning] has taught us that one initiative in an institution creates ripple effects in other parts . . . effecting systemic change. As a result of our campus conversations [about the scholarship of teaching and learning] we are . . . beginning to convert catchphrases like "the importance of teaching" and "teaching institution" from vague slogans into affirmations of the value of teaching and learning as institutional priorities. (Albert, Moore, and Mincey, 2004, p. 192)

An Integrative Vision

As readers of this volume know well, many promising reform efforts in higher education fail to make a long-term difference. This happens for many reasons, but one, certainly, can be that the effort's very success—its ability to attract a group of practitioners and champions—creates a kind of silo or cult, separate from the ongoing work of the institution. I will confess that I have worried, at times, that this might be the fate of the scholarship of teaching and learning. The challenge is to weave this "movement" into the ongoing rhythms of academic life and institutions; to move from "catch-phrases" . . . to "systemic change," as the quote above suggests.

Moving toward this kind of transformation has been a hallmark of recent developments in the scholarship of teaching and learning, as campus leaders have found ways to harness its principles and practices to larger, shared agendas and institutional priorities. To be clear, the engagement of individual faculty exploring their own students' learning and sharing what they learn with others who can build on it will likely (and rightly) continue to be the *sine qua non* and prime mover of this work. However, it is now possible to see such efforts converging around more collective agendas, whether by happenstance, as scholars pursuing similar questions and goals discover one another and find ways to pool their efforts, or by design, where the scholarship of teaching and learning is framed from the outset as a road toward larger changes.

Examples of this more collaborative, cross-cutting approach are now multiplying, for instance in the form of collections of work by scholars of teaching and learning in different settings but organized around a common theme (see, for example, Garung, Chick, and Haynie, 2008; Smith, Nowacek, and Bernstein, 2010). The Visible Knowledge Project, a multi-campus scholarship of teaching and learning effort involving faculty in history and cultural studies, resulted in powerful webs of influence and knowledge building in which projects were informed by one another (Bass and Eynon, 2009). Within CASTL, a group of campuses joined forces to use the scholarship of teaching and learning to improve their approaches to undergraduate research (Beckman and Hensel, 2009). And a number of campuses are exploring fruitful intersections between the scholarship of teaching and learning, assessment, and accreditation, as well (Cambridge, 2004; Ciccone, Huber, Hutchings, and Cambridge, 2009).

Developments like these reflect an understanding of the scholarship of teaching and learning not as a discrete activity or approach but as a way of thinking about the ongoing work of teaching and learning: a vision in which faculty habits and values as scholars are brought to bear on their interactions with students. Indeed, one of the most powerful lessons of this work over recent years has been the value of involving students—both undergraduate and graduate—by inviting them into this work not (or not only) as objects of study, but as participants in exploring and shaping their own learning. Such involvement has been the guiding principle of a growing group of institutions that collaborated to describe their experiences of (as the title of their volume says) *Engaging Student Voices in the Study of Teaching and Learning* (Werder and Otis, 2010). In some settings this has meant involvement in curricular reform; in others, participation in powerful discussion with all members of the academic community, or engagement in forms of undergraduate research that are explicitly focused on the learning experience. For many students, these experiences are transformational. As one of them noted, "it flipped a switch, and once it's flipped it can't be turned off" (quoted in Huber and Hutchings, 2005). This student is now a teacher.

The scholarship of teaching and learning is a work in progress. It is built on the "big idea" that teaching, like learning, is intellectual work, work that can be improved through systematic inquiry, critique, and collaboration within a diverse community of learners, be they teachers or students; indeed, it strives to make better learners of both. Such a shift can be strange or even scary for those brought up in an academic culture that has treated pedagogy as a private enterprise, to be conducted behind closed doors—and it is not without risks. But the risks come with significant benefits, for when our work as educators is undertaken in a spirit of curiosity, intellectual honesty, and generosity, *new* new directions for teaching and learning will surely emerge.

References

Albert, L. S., Moore, M. R., and Mincey, K. C. "An Ongoing Journey." In B. Cambridge (ed.), *Campus Progress: Supporting the Scholarship of Teaching and Learning.* Washington, D.C.: American Association for Higher Education, 2004.

Angelo, T. A., and Cross, K. P. *Classroom Assessment Techniques: A Handbook for College Teachers.* San Francisco: Jossey-Bass, 1993.

Bass, R. "The Scholarship of Teaching and Learning: What's the Problem?" *Inventio: Creative Thinking About Learning and Teaching,* 1999, *1*(1). [http://www.doit.gmu.edu/Archives/feb98/randybasshtm].

Bass, R., and Eynon, B. (eds.). "The Difference That Inquiry Makes: A Collaborative Case Study of Technology and Learning, from the Visible Knowledge Project." *Academic Commons,* 2009. [http://www.academiccommons.org/issue/january-2009].

Beckman, M., and Hensel, N. "Making Explicit the Implicit: Defining Undergraduate Research." *Council on Undergraduate Research,* 2009, *29*(4), 40–44. www.cur.org.

Bernstein, D., Burnett, A. N., Goodburn, A., and Savory, P. *Making Teaching and Learning Visible: Course Portfolios and the Peer Review of Teaching.* Bolton, Mass.: Anker, 2006.

Boyer, E. *Scholarship Reconsidered: Priorities of the Professoriate.* Princeton, N.J.: The Carnegie Foundation for the Advancement of Teaching, 1990.

Cambridge, B. L. (ed.). *Campus Progress: Supporting the Scholarship of Teaching and Learning.* Washington, D.C.: American Association for Higher Education, 2004.

Ciccone, A. "Furthering the Scholarship of Teaching and Learning the Wisconsin Way." In B. Cambridge (ed.), *Campus Progress: Supporting the Scholarship of Teaching and Learning.* Washington, D.C.: American Association for Higher Education, 2004.

Ciccone, A. "CASTL's 'Big Bang' Distributes SOTL Far and Wide." *International Society for the Scholarship of Teaching and Learning International Commons,* 2009, *4*(3), 10. [www.issotl.org/history.html].

Ciccone, A., Huber, M. T., Hutchings, P., and Cambridge, B. "Exploring Impact: A Survey of Participants in the CASTL Institutional Leadership and Affiliates Program." Unpublished paper. The Carnegie Foundation for the Advancement of Teaching, Stanford, Calif., 2009.

Cochran-Smith, M., and Lytle, S. "The Teacher Research Movement: A Decade Later." *Educational Researcher,* 1999, *28*(7), 15–25.

Diamond, R. M., and Adam, B. E. (eds.). *The Disciplines Speak: Rewarding the Scholarly, Professional, and Creative Work of Faculty.* Washington, D.C.: American Association for Higher Education, 1995.

Gale, R. "Points Without Limits: Individual Inquiry, Collaborative Investigation, and Collective Scholarship." *To Improve the Academy, Vol. 26, pp. 39–52.* October 2007.

Garung, R., Chick, N., and Haynie, A. (eds.). *Exploring Signature Pedagogies: Approaches to Teaching Disciplinary Habits of Mind.* Sterling, Va.: Stylus, 2008.

Healey, M. "Developing the Scholarship of Teaching and Learning in Higher Education: A Discipline-Based Approach." *Higher Education Research & Development,* 2002, 19(2), 169–189.

Huber, M. T. *Balancing Acts: The Scholarship of Teaching and Learning in Academic Careers.* Washington, D.C.: American Association for Higher Education and The Carnegie Foundation for the Advancement of Teaching, 2004.

Huber, M. T. "CASTL Has Concluded. Long Live the Scholarship of Teaching and Learning!" *Arts and Humanities in Higher Education,* 2010, 9(1), 5–7.

Huber, M. T., and Hutchings, P. *The Advancement of Learning: Building the Teaching Commons.* San Francisco: Jossey-Bass, 2005.

Huber, M. T., and Morreale, S. P. (eds.). *Disciplinary Styles in the Scholarship of Teaching and Learning: Exploring Common Ground.* Washington, D.C.: American Association for Higher Education and The Carnegie Foundation for the Advancement of Teaching, 2002.

Hutchings, P. (ed.). *Making Teaching Community Property: A Menu for Peer Collaboration and Peer Review.* Washington, D.C.: American Association for Higher Education, 1996.

Hutchings, P., and Huber, M. T. "Placing Theory in the Scholarship of Teaching and Learning." *Arts and Humanities in Higher Education,* 2008, 7(3), 229–244.

Hutchings, P., and Shulman, L. S. "The Scholarship of Teaching: New Elaborations, New Developments." *Change,* 1999, 31(5), 10–15.

International Society for the Scholarship of Teaching and Learning. "History." [www.issotl.org/history.html].

Kreber, C. "Conceptualizing the Scholarship of Teaching and Identifying Unresolved Issues: The Framework for This Volume." In C. Kreber (ed.), *Revisiting Scholarship: Perspectives on the Scholarship of Teaching and Learning.* New Directions for Teaching and Learning, no. 86. San Francisco: Jossey-Bass, 2001.

McKeachie, W. J. (ed.). *Learning, Cognition, and College Teaching.* New Directions for Teaching and Learning, no. 2. San Francisco: Jossey-Bass, 1980.

McKinney, K. *Enhancing Learning Through the Scholarship of Teaching and Learning: The Challenges and Joys of Juggling.* San Francisco: Jossey-Bass, 2007.

O'Meara, K., and Rice, R. E. (eds.). *Faculty Priorities Reconsidered: Rewarding Multiple Forms of Scholarship.* San Francisco: Jossey-Bass with the American Association for Higher Education, 2005.

Pace, D. "The Amateur in the Operating Room: History and the Scholarship of Teaching and Learning." *American Historical Review,* 2004, 109(4), 1171–1192.

Post, C. J. "Promotion and Tenure Track Record." In B. Cambridge (ed.), *Campus Progress: Supporting the Scholarship of Teaching and Learning.* Washington, D.C.: American Association for Higher Education, 2004.

Roen, D. "Introduction." In B. Cambridge (ed.), *Campus Progress: Supporting the Scholarship of Teaching and Learning.* Washington, D.C.: American Association for Higher Education, 2004.

Roxä, T., Olsson, T., and Märtensson, K. "Appropriate Use of Theory in the Scholarship of Teaching and Learning as a Strategy for Institutional Development." *Arts and Humanities in Higher Education,* 2008, 7(3), 276–294.

Schön, D. A. *The Reflective Practitioner: How Professionals Think in Action.* New York: Basic Books, 1983.

Shulman, L. S. "Knowledge and Teaching: Foundations of the New Reform." *Harvard Educational Review,* 1987, 57(1), 1–22.

Shulman, L. S. "The Wisdom of Practice: Managing Complexity and Medicine and

Teaching." In S. Wilson (ed.), *The Wisdom of Practice: Essays on Teaching, Learning, and Learning to Teach*. San Francisco: Jossey-Bass, 2004. (Originally published in 1987.)

Smith, M. B., Nowacek, R. S., and Bernstein, J. L. *Citizenship Across the Curriculum*. Bloomington, Ind.: Indiana University Press, 2010.

Tinberg, H., Duffy, D. K., and Mino, J. "The Scholarship of Teaching and Learning at the Two-Year College: Promise and Peril." *Change*, 2007, *39*(4), 226–233.

Trigwell, K. "Student Learning and the Scholarship of Teaching and Learning." Keynote Speech at the International Society for the Scholarship of Teaching and Learning Inaugural Conference, Indiana University, Bloomington, Ind., October 21, 2004.

Werder, C., and Otis, M. M. (eds.). *Engaging Student Voices in the Study of Teaching and Learning*. Sterling, Va.: Stylus, 2010.

PAT HUTCHINGS *is a senior associate with The Carnegie Foundation for the Advancement of Teaching, where she previously served as vice president and as senior scholar, providing leadership for the decade-long Carnegie Academy for the Scholarship of Teaching and Learning. She has written widely on the investigation and documentation of teaching and learning, the peer collaboration and review of teaching, and the scholarship of teaching and learning. Recent publications include* Ethics of Inquiry: Issues in the Scholarship of Teaching and Learning *(2002),* Opening Lines: Approaches to the Scholarship of Teaching and Learning *(2000), and, co-authored with Mary Taylor Huber,* The Advancement of Learning: Building the Teaching Commons *(2005). She was chair of the English department at Alverno College from 1978 to 1987 and a senior staff member at the American Association for Higher Education from 1987–1997.*

NEW DIRECTIONS FOR TEACHING AND LEARNING • DOI: 10.1002/tl

*This chapter discusses how far the field of Self-Regulated Learning
has come since the mid-1990s based on the work started by Paul
Pintrich. The growth in understanding of why self-regulated
learning is important to teaching and learning is outlined and
Pintrich's model is presented and discussed.*

Student Learning: From Teacher-Directed to Self-Regulation

Marilla D. Svinicki

In 1995 when *New Directions* issue No. 63, *Understanding Self-Regulated
Learning*, was published, the issue editor, Paul Pintrich, was one of the
leaders in studying how college students learn and what helps or hinders
them during the process. His contributions to the field have been tremendous and very significant both theoretically and pragmatically. His
untimely death from a stroke in 2003 robbed the field of someone who was
destined to bring many insights into how students develop as self-regulated
learners. This chapter is a tribute to how far the field has come since the
mid-nineties, and much of the progress builds on and continues the work
started by Pintrich. His work continued to be published posthumously and
still leads the field. It is an honor to compile these ideas and present them
to a new generation of faculty.

The Original Issue

In 1995 Pintrich laid out the components of self-regulation that were considered key to self-regulation, based on the research at that time. Those
three keys have held up well across the years and continued investigations.
I draw from his words here (Pintrich, 1995, p. 5):

1. "... self-regulated learners attempt to *control* their behavior, motivation and affect, and cognition."
2. "... there is some *goal* the student is attempting to accomplish ..."

NEW DIRECTIONS FOR TEACHING AND LEARNING, no. 123, Fall 2010 © Wiley Periodicals, Inc.
View this article online at wileyonlinelibrary.com. • DOI: 10.1002/tl.411

3. ". . . *the individual student*—not someone else like a parent or teacher—must be in control of his actions."

The key for Pintrich and others in distinguishing a self-regulated learner was in that personal control of their behavior and environment. As noted in the title to this chapter, the shift was being made from teacher control and responsibility for learning to learner control and personal responsibility. This sentiment was echoed in another very influential article published at that same time by Barr and Tagg (1995) that encouraged higher education to move from a teaching to a learning paradigm to enhance the effectiveness of higher education. That sentiment to move toward a learner-centered focus has since become a cornerstone of a lot of change in the way courses are taught and evaluated.

An important caveat to making this connection is that this paradigm shift was not exactly what the educational psychology field meant by self-regulation, however. In the learner-centered paradigm, the focus was definitely on the learner, but not to the extent that the learner exercised control. Rather, although the instruction followed the learners' progress and was centered on the learners' skills and needs and to some extent was guided by the learners, the instructional designer was still in control. The self-regulation movement took that focus on the learner one step further by locating the control and responsibility for learning squarely on the learners' shoulders.

For Pintrich (1995; Boekaerts, Pintrich, and Zeidner, 2000) and others working in learning psychology, this was an important distinction and was grounded in the rise of constructivist views of learning, which had replaced behaviorism and, to some extent, information-processing theory, as the dominant model of learning for that period. The constructivist model asserts that during learning, the learner "constructs" his or her understanding of the environment from his or her interactions with it rather than the environment creating new stimulus-response connections. As a consequence, each learner constructs a unique (though similar) view of the world and how it works. The learner truly is in charge of learning. The instructor simply helps the learner by providing a rich environment from which the learner can learn.

Another important theory of learning that was developing at the same time with complementary interpretations of learning was social cognitive theory, spearheaded by Bandura (1989). In social cognitive theory, a very large component is the idea of individual agency. The learner was viewed as the agent of change in his or her own behavior. This perspective gave strong theoretical support for the notion of self-regulation, not just in learning, but in all forms of human behavior.

Although self-regulation is more than constructivism or social cognitive theory, it definitely is consistent with the notion that it is the learner that is doing the work during learning. Self-regulation theory expanded on

NEW DIRECTIONS FOR TEACHING AND LEARNING • DOI: 10.1002/tl

that initial step in the learning process by attempting to specify what the learner could and does do to control that learning process. In self-regulation theory learners working toward their goals marshal the cognitive strategies available to them to make their learning more efficient and effective. Another key idea in self-regulation is that these monitoring and control skills can be enhanced through instruction. Learners can learn to monitor and manipulate the way they go about learning once they become aware of what they are doing. This is the goal of self-regulation training: to enhance learners' control over their own learning.

Hearkening back to his original definition and adding a new wrinkle, Pintrich (2000) summarized the various theories of self-regulation at the time as control processes revolving around behavior, motivation and affect, and cognition, and adding control over the context. The behavior aspect of the processes involves monitoring what you are *doing* that results in progress toward the goal—things like self-observation of behavior, monitoring effort expenditure, seeking help when it is needed, and planning for action. The motivation and affect aspects involve actions such as setting goals that are reasonable and valuable, and monitoring emotional states to make sure that frustration or distractions do not sidetrack progress. The cognitive aspect involves setting goals, drawing on prior knowledge, awareness of and monitoring thinking, checking understanding, summarizing what has been working or not working, and, possibly most important of all, making appropriate attributions about what is driving outcomes. Control over the context involves being aware of the demands of the task, the resources available to assist learning, strategies for modifying the task or environment to facilitate learning, and monitoring changes in the context that might affect learning. In this particular summary of research and theory, Pintrich also charted four phases of self-regulated learning: (1) planning, (2) monitoring, (3) exercising control, and (4) reaction and reflection. At each of these four phases, there are appropriate actions for the four areas of control just described: (1) cognition, (2) motivation/affect, (3) behavior, and (4) context. This model of self-regulation is shown in summary in Figure 8.1.

The model could be used to help learners develop their learning effectiveness by adding the appropriate strategies for each to their repertoire. A much more detailed version of this model and Figure 8.1 is provided by Pintrich (2004). That article, published posthumously, provides suggestions

Figure 8.1. Pintrich (2004) Model of Phases and Areas for Self-Regulated Learning

Phases/Areas for Regulation	Cognition	Motivation/Affect	Behavior	Context
Planning				
Monitoring				
Control				
Reaction and Reflection				

about the kinds of actions that can occur in each of the cells of the model. In addition Pintrich discusses the development of instruments (in particular, his own Motivated Strategies for Learning Questionnaire [MSLQ]) to assess learners' use of those actions, which can help learners identify strengths and weaknesses, and take steps to remedy the latter. This instrument has since become a staple in research on learning. Although far from being the only model of self-regulation that was suggested over the years (see Boekaerts, Pintrich, and Zeidner, 2000; Zimmerman and Schunk, 2008), Pintrich's model had developed in depth and detail from the original description of it in the *New Directions* issue he edited in 1995.

Where Has Self-Regulation Gone Since Then?

The development of theory for self-regulated learning has not stood still since the publishing of the *New Directions* issue. For example, the questions being asked now have become far more sophisticated. In a recent review by Azevedo (2009) as part of a special issue on self-regulated learning, the author highlights some of the current questions that are facing those who try to study self-regulation and metacognition (that aspect of regulation that focuses on monitoring and controlling thinking).

Measuring Self-Regulation. There are, of course, always measurement questions about researching such an internal process. Even after all this time, there is not universal agreement on what constitutes self-regulated learning. Should one be studying macroprocesses, such as large-scale goal setting, or microprocesses, such as in the moment strategy use? In the same collection of articles, Schraw (2009) compares the instruments that exist for measuring student self-regulation and illustrates how they represent different perspectives on the subject. Without good measures it becomes difficult to reconcile research findings. One solution proposed by Schraw is to use all the measures simultaneously until their interrelationships can be teased out of the data. So, even after all this time, a task for theorists and researchers is to find a coherent definition that all can agree on to guide future studies. No one disagrees that self-regulation is an important phenomenon to study; there is just more sophisticated disagreement on what components are most potent in helping students learn.

Connecting with Other Theories. The concept of self-regulation has been joined by two important motivation theories to add weight to the importance of control by the learner. Motivation theory in the 1990s and beyond has focused on two interesting task characteristics that definitely influence an individual's self-regulation propensities. The first of these two motivation theories was proposed by Ryan and Deci (2000) and is referred to as self-determination theory. In this theory, individuals are said to be motivated by three basic needs: autonomy, competence, and relatedness. The latter two needs are not as relevant to self-regulation (but not irrelevant), but it is the idea of autonomy that matches up with theories of self-regulation. Ryan and Deci suggested that individuals needed to feel as if they were in control of their world, that their actions were self-determined rather than determined by external forces. Those feelings of autonomy then lead to higher levels of motivation for a task, even if the task is not itself motivating. This assertion is obviously relevant to the idea of self-regulation. When students are able to exercise self-regulation, they feel more in control of their learning and hence more motivated to perform.

The second motivation theory that fits with self-regulation was proposed by Elliott and Dweck (1988), along with several other researchers working in the same time frame (Ames, 1992; Maehr and Midgley, 1991; Nicholls, 1984; for more details, see Pintrich and Schunk, 2002). These theories all propose that motivation and its expression are both influenced by the types of goals that learners are working toward and their orientation toward those goals. Specifically, they suggest that sometimes learners choose to work toward mastery of a task—described as learning as much as possible without worrying about errors or appearances. Sometimes learners are working under a performance orientation—described as the desire to appear competent or at least avoid looking incompetent. There are many variations on these themes, but the difference between working toward an internally evaluated goal versus an externally evaluated goal is probably the most prominent aspect of these theories. What is their importance for self-regulation? Because one of the aspects of self-regulation is the identification of goals and strategies for achieving them, an understanding of the attitudes and behaviors associated with different goal orientations is quite relevant. In general, mastery goal orientation is more associated with using quality learning strategies and greater motivation, whereas performance goal orientation is more associated with what in the literature is called "shallow learning" and tenuous motivation. Therefore, it would be beneficial to encourage students to adopt a mastery orientation in their self-regulation regimen by creating a safe environment for learning in which errors are treated as learning opportunities and students feel supported by their instructor and their peers.

An Increased Focus on Components.

Emotions. The second area where more has been learned about self-regulation involves an increased focus on components of the process, especially regulation of emotion and beliefs that support learning. The emotion area has begun to receive a great deal more attention in the educational literature in the last few years, but the awareness that emotion impacts learning has been in the literature for a long time. Most prominent has been the relationship between anxiety and learning. Known as the Yerkes Dodson effect (for the researchers who studied it), anxiety has a curvilinear relationship with arousal/anxiety. Very low levels of arousal/anxiety are associated with low levels of performance. Very high levels of anxiety are associated with low levels of performance also. And somewhere in the middle is the optimal level of arousal, which produces an optimal level of performance. In educational settings this relationship is seen in conditions such as test anxiety, math anxiety, performance anxiety, and writer's block. Many practical methods for controlling anxiety have been developed over the years, several drawn from counseling theories. In the last twenty years theories and research on *academic* emotion and its impacts on learning have become more prominent (Pekrun, 1992). In general these theories and solutions are very similar in form to the kinds of strategies involved in self-regulation. For example, Bembenutty (2009) studied the interrelationship between self-regulated learning and text anxiety and the impact each has on student achievement, and suggests that instructors need to work with students on both types of regulation: cognitive as well as affective (anxiety). On the other hand, Turner and Husman (2008), in studying how students deal with the emotional aspects of learning, suggested that having an array of study and motivational strategies was helpful in mitigating the impact of stressful emotions. The implications might be that it is the knowledge that one *can* recognize emotional potholes and purposefully steer around them that reduces the anxiety associated with academic evaluation.

Beliefs About Learning. In addition to the array of cognitive strategies for regulating learning, the impact of beliefs about learning is being investigated for their impact on use of those strategies. Paulsen and Feldman (2007) studied the effects of four beliefs about learning on different types of self-regulation skills, including both cognitive strategies and behavioral strategies. They found that students with more sophisticated beliefs about learning (for example, "learning doesn't happen instantly," "knowledge is not a fixed commodity," and so on) tended also to use both cognitive and behavioral strategies more effectively. Of the beliefs they tested, beliefs about the fixed nature of ability had the biggest impact on self-regulation: the greater the belief in the possibility for changes in ability through effort, the more effective the use of self-regulation. The authors describe their findings like this:

> . . . holding naive beliefs that one's ability to learn is fixed at birth and cannot be improved reduces the likelihood that a student will consider it worthwhile to engage in potentially educationally productive cognitive strategies in their learning—including both surface-level processing strategies (rehearsal) and deep-level processing strategies (elaboration, organization and metacognition). . . . (p. 382)

The authors report the same findings for the behaviorally based strategies, such as managing time and environment, seeking help from others, and regulating effort. An earlier study by Paulsen and Feldman (2005) reported similar effects on the use of motivational self-regulation. This phenomenon is discussed at length in Dweck (2006), who offers several examples of the belief about ability being fixed from birth versus changeable through effort, making a compelling argument about the importance of beliefs in motivation and achievement.

Search for Interventions to Enhance Self-Regulated Learning. Throughout the growth of the self-regulated learning literature, one conundrum has remained unresolved. If self-regulation is such a good skill, why don't more students take advantage of it? Actually, as Hofer, Yu, and Pintrich (1998) note, there isn't much known about how self-regulation is learned naturally, much less taught specifically. When asked, most of us just shrug our shoulders and say that we don't remember how we learned it. However, the hope that there is a way to induce self-regulation in learners remains high. Hofer, Yu, and Pintrich wrote in the early days of the movement that four questions needed to be addressed when planning for instruction in self-regulation: what to teach, whom to teach, whether to do it within the context of a content course or as a separate, stand-alone course, and finally how to encourage students to transfer what they learned to other settings. At the conclusion of their article, the authors admitted that they did not yet have an answer to those questions.

Unfortunately that still holds true for today: The answer isn't clear. However, progress is being made. For example, there seems to be fairly widespread agreement among practitioners that the "what" of instruction should include all aspects of self-regulation: cognitive, motivation/affective, behavior, and context management.

Help Seeking. Another body of research related to the what-to-teach question focuses on help seeking. How do we help students learn when it is appropriate to ask for help? An early aspect of this work by Karabenick and Knapp (1991) illustrated that an important component of this effort is the need to change the view of help seeking from a dependent behavior to a strategic behavior. They found in a series of studies that active learners were more likely to seek help when they needed it than students who were more passive in their use of learning strategies. Removing the stigma of dependency could remove one barrier to this self-regulation activity. Later research by the same team looked at the course variables that influenced help seeking and found that student perceptions of the structure of the class (is the emphasis on grades or learning?) as well as the real conditions within a class (such as size) impacted help-seeking (Karabenick, 2004). They conclude that the perception of need was a critical factor in convincing students to seek help.

Calibration of Understanding. The concept of perception of need raises another issue currently being studied in this literature: student calibration of need. By calibration, researchers mean the accuracy of a student's perception of the demands of a task, the skill and knowledge level he or she brings to the task, and the quality of his or her performance of the task (Bembenutty, 2009). From all aspects of self-regulation the ability to recognize the degree to which one is accurate in assessing progress is a critical step.

NEW DIRECTIONS FOR TEACHING AND LEARNING • DOI: 10.1002/tl

Feedback from Self and Others. One important source of learning of this skill is the kind of feedback that a student receives, which is another stream of research in the literature. Nicol and Macfarlane-Dick (2005) make a strong case for providing more frequent formative feedback, but add that it is more important to help the learner take control of the feedback process himself or herself. Until the learner is in control of feedback, it is hard to claim that he or she is self-regulating. Therefore, Nicol and Macfarlane-Dick (2005) offer seven practices of formative feedback that should improve its usefulness to a learner. Those practices in brief are:

1. Clarifying what "good" performance is by making goals and criteria clear
2. Facilitating the development of self-assessment through reflection activities embedded during learning
3. Providing high-quality diagnostic information about the student's learning
4. Giving opportunities for dialogue about learning with peers or the instructor
5. Fostering positive motivation and self-efficacy
6. Providing opportunities to practice and improve
7. Providing information to the teacher about how to change teaching to help students

Technology That Provides Support. One of the new possibilities for developing self-regulation involves the use of technology. Although there were discussions about the similarity between hypermedia and individual thought processes even in the 1990s (Anderson, Corbett, Koedinger, and Pelletier, 1995), most of the advances in the use of computer-based tutors (intelligent tutors) have been in the decade between 2000 and 2009. For example, Winne and others (2006) report on the development of a software system that incorporates cognitive tools that are based on the concepts of self-regulation behaviors. By building into the instructional presentation tools that allow students to set goals, take notes, monitor their understanding, and other components of self-regulation, the authors are hoping to make these skills so easy to use that their use becomes an integral part of the student's learning repertoire. The most prolific researcher in this area is Azevedo, who, with a series of collaborators, has provided a great deal of insight into the ability of hypermedia to scaffold self-regulation (Azevedo and Hadwin, 2005; Jacobson and Azevedo, 2008; Moos and Azevedo, 2008). This use of technology holds a great deal of promise in helping students to develop self-regulation skills.

What Does It All Mean for Self-Regulation?

As is the case in many educational areas, what we have learned most definitely since the first *New Directions* issue on self-regulation is that what

NEW DIRECTIONS FOR TEACHING AND LEARNING • DOI: 10.1002/tl

may have seemed fairly straightforward in 1995, isn't. The more we learn about self-regulation the more there is to learn. However, I believe it is safe to assert the following:

1. Self-regulation of learning has been demonstrated to improve performance; therefore, its development is worth both the student's and the instructor's time.
2. Self-regulation is a complex set of skills with many components. It involves more than the control over thinking and behavior; it also requires attention to motivation, emotions, and beliefs that affect the learner's perception of the possible.
3. Self-regulation can be learned, although it is difficult, which sometimes deters students from being willing to take the time to develop it.
4. Self-regulation is a skill learned through direct instruction paired with overt modeling by an instructor through the course of learning.
5. Providing self-regulation prompts in student assignments increases the probability that it will occur, but doesn't necessarily increase student independent use of the skills being prompted. The student may not be able to differentiate between the context and the skills.
6. Embedding training in self-regulation in real courses improves student motivation for it, but may hinder transfer. Teaching the skills in the context of a separate course can affect motivation and ability to use the skills in real contexts.

For now, it seems most reasonable for instructors to return to the model that Pintrich proposed in 2000, which is represented in Figure 8.1 in this chapter. The model still serves as a reasonable source of ideas about self-regulation for both teachers and students. The work since it was developed has been to refine the contents of the cells, but not to change the big picture about self-regulation that the model offers.

References

Ames, C. "Classrooms: Goals, Structures, and Student Motivation." *Journal of Educational Psychology*, 1992, *84*, 261–271.

Anderson, J., Corbett, A., Koedinger, K., and Pelletier, R. "Cognitive Tutors: Lessons Learned." *Journal of the Learning Sciences*, 1995, *4*(2), 167–207.

Azevedo, R. "Theoretical, Conceptual, Methodological, and Instruction Issues in Research on Metacognition and Self-Regulated Learning: A Discussion." *Metacognition and Learning*, 2009, *4*, 87–95.

Azevedo, R., and Hadwin, A. "Scaffolding Self-Regulated Learning and Metacognition—Implications for the Design of Computer-Based Scaffolds." *Instructional Science*, 2005, *33*, 367–379.

Bandura, A. "Human Agency in Social Cognitive Theory." *The American Psychologist*, 1989, *44*(9), 1175–1185.

Barr, R., and Tagg, J. "From Teaching to Learning—A New Paradigm for Undergraduate Education." *Change*, 1995, *27*(6), 12–14.

Bembenutty, H. "Three Essential Components of College Teaching: Achievement Calibration, Self-Efficacy, and Self-Regulation." *College Student Journal, Part B,* 2009, *43*(2), 562–570.

Boekaerts, M., Pintrich, P., and Zeidner, M. *Handbook of Self-Regulation.* San Diego, CA: Academic Press, 2000.

Dweck, C. *Mindset: The New Psychology of Success.* New York: Random House, 2006.

Elliott, E., and Dweck, C. "Goals: An Approach to Motivation and Achievement." *Journal of Personality and Social Psychology,* 1988, *54,* 5–12.

Hofer, B., Yu, S., and Pintrich, P. "Teaching College Students to Be Self-Regulated Learners." In D. Schunk and B. D. Zimmerman (eds.), *Self-Regulated Learning: From Teaching to Self-Reflective Practice.* New York: Guilford Press, 1998, pp. 57–85.

Jacobson, M., and Azevedo, R. "Advances in Scaffolding Learning with Hypertext and Hypermedia: Theoretical, Empirical, and Design Issues." *Educational Technology Research and Development,* 2008, *56,* 1–3.

Karabenick, S. "Perceived Achievement Goal Structure and College Student Help Seeking." *Journal of Educational Psychology,* 2004, *96*(3), 569–581.

Karabenick, S., and Knapp, J. "Relationship of Academic Help Seeking to the Use of Learning Strategies and Other Instrumental Achievement Behavior in College Students." *Journal of Educational Psychology,* 1991, *83*(7), 221–230.

Maehr, M., and Midgley, C. "Enhancing Student Motivation: A Schoolwide Approach." *Educational Psychologist,* 1991, *26,* 399–427.

Moos, D., and Azevedo, R. "Monitoring, Planning, and Self-Efficacy During Learning with Hypermedia: The Impact of Conceptual Scaffolds." *Computers in Human Behavior,* 2008, *24,* 1686–1706.

Nicol, D., and Macfarlane-Dick, D. "Formative Assessment and Self-Regulated Learning: A Model and Seven Principles of Good Feedback Practice." *Studies in Higher Education,* Vol. 31(2), 2005, 199–2005.

Nicholls, J. "Achievement Motivation: Conceptions of Ability, Subjective Experience, Task Choice, and Performance." *Psychological Review,* 1984, *91,* 328–346.

Paulsen, M., and Feldman, K. "The Conditional and Interaction Effects of Epistemological Beliefs on the Self-Regulated Learning of College Students: Motivational Strategies." *Research in Higher Education,* 2005, *46*(7), 731–768.

Paulsen, M., and Feldman, K. "The Conditional and Interaction Effects of Epistemological Beliefs on the Self-Regulated Learning of College Students: Cognitive and Behavioral Strategies." *Research in Higher Education,* 2007, *48*(3), 353–401.

Pekrun, R. "The Impact of Emotions on Learning and Achievement: Towards a Theory of Cognitive/Motivational Mediators." *Applied Psychology: An International Review,* 1992, *41,* 359–376.

Pintrich, P. *Understanding Self-Regulated Learning.* New Directions for Teaching and Learning, no. 63. San Francisco: Jossey-Bass, 1995.

Pintrich, P. "The Role of Goal Orientation in Self-Regulated Learning." In M. Boekaerts, P. Pintrich, and M. Zeidner (eds.), *Handbook of Self-Regulation.* San Diego, CA: Academic Press, 2000, pp. 452–500.

Pintrich, P. "A Conceptual Framework for Assessing Motivation and Self-Regulated Learning in College Students." *Educational Psychology Review,* 2004, *16*(4), 385–407.

Pintrich, P., and Schunk, D. *Motivation in Education: Theory, Research, and Applications.* Upper Saddle River, N.J.: Merrill, Prentice Hall, 2002.

Ryan, R., and Deci, E. "Intrinsic and Extrinsic Motivations: Classic Definitions and New Directions." *Contemporary Educational Psychology,* 2000, *25,* 54–67.

Schraw, G. "A Conceptual Analysis of Five Measures of Metacognitive Monitoring." *Metacognition and Learning,* 2009, *4,* 33–45.

Turner, J., and Husman, J. "Emotional and Cognitive Self-Regulation Following Academic Shame." *Journal of Advanced Academics,* 2008, *20*(1), 138–173.

Winne, P., Nesbit, J., Kumar, V., Hadwin, A., Lajoie, S., Azevedo, R., and Perry, N. "Supporting Self-Regulated Learning with Study Software: The Learning Kit Project." *Technology, Instruction, Cognition and Learning,* 2006, *3,* 105–113.

Zimmerman, B. J., and Schunk, D. H. (eds.). *Self-Regulated Learning and Academic Achievement: Theoretical Perspectives.* (2nd ed.) Mahwah, N.J.: Lawrence Erlbaum, 2008, pp. 153–189.

MARILLA D. SVINICKI is a professor of educational psychology at the University of Texas at Austin and former director of the Center for Teaching Effectiveness at the same institution. She has been active in faculty development since 1973 and served for two terms as the executive director of the POD Network.

NEW DIRECTIONS FOR TEACHING AND LEARNING • DOI: 10.1002/tl

9

The evaluation of teaching has sparked much debate for many decades. This chapter explores the many uses of teaching evaluations and suggests directions for how to best use the information that is gained.

Evaluating Teaching: From Reliability to Accountability

Michael Theall

In the Beginning

In the 1960s, research on faculty evaluation was already more than thirty years old. Remmers and Brandenburg (1927) had begun to explore student ratings of instruction much earlier, but interest in evaluation was now building rapidly. Some attribute the increased interest, and especially the growth of student ratings of instruction, to social unrest and the rise of a more demanding student population, one that wanted a voice in decisions about the effectiveness of faculty. But there were other reasons. Higher education institutions were feeling the pressures of competition for students, and they desired more information with which to demonstrate the quality of teaching, curricular programs, and student success. At the same time, technological progress made statistical analysis of large data sets more efficient and economical, and given the roots of evaluation in measurement and psychometrics, there was great interest in establishing the technical characteristics of instruments used in evaluation, as well as interest in creating the foundation of the field of evaluation from practical and philosophical perspectives. Cronbach (1963) discussed "Course Improvement Through Evaluation." Taylor and Maguire (1966) proposed "A Theoretical Evaluation Model." Scriven (1967) authored a "Methodology of Evaluation," suggesting that the goals of evaluation were always to provide judgments of merit or worth. Scriven also originated terms for the roles of evaluation ("formative and summative") that are still used today, and identified two kinds of evaluation data: "instrumental" (process data) and "consequential" (outcome data). Stake (1968) disagreed to some extent about the judgmental role of evaluation, but noted that evaluation should look for congruence between intended and observed results in terms of antecedents (preexisting conditions), transactions (activities), and outcomes (specified performance targets determined by those who develop programs).

The overlap between these efforts and the field of faculty evaluation is clear in the sense that before the 1960s, faculty were primarily responsible for developing courses and curricula, providing instruction, and assessing student learning, with their performance judged primarily by their department chairs and colleagues. The distinction between instrumental and consequential data became an important issue when it became clear that instrumental data were easily and effectively collected through the use of validated student surveys, and outcomes data were largely drawn from traditional, nonstandardized classroom measures like tests and grades. Two issues were apparent: (1) analyses of large data sets of student ratings of instruction were possible to establish reliability and validity of the survey instruments and processes used, but (2) opportunities to validate classroom tests were many fewer and much more restricted. The evidence at hand became the evidence of choice.

Paradigm Shifts Occur and Accountability Demands Increase

Prior to the 1960s, the predominant teaching paradigm was tied to a consensus that a principal function of higher education was to separate those who had the ability to successfully pursue a college degree from those who did not. Thus, although the responsibility for teaching (transmission of information) fell to the faculty, the responsibility for learning (acquisition of knowledge and skills) was largely placed on the shoulders of the students. If a teacher possessed characteristics or did things considered to be good (for example, being knowledgeable of the content or delivering well-organized lectures), that teacher was effective. It was sometimes the case that good teaching was equated with failing a considerable number of students: this was evidence of having consistently high standards and preserving the quality of the discipline or profession. The sixties were a turning point with respect to the start of a paradigm shift that did not fully occur until late in the century (Barr and Tagg, 1995). One major and significant difference in the fifty years that transpired is that much more responsibility for learning was passed to the faculty. This is encapsulated in the commonly heard question, "If there is no learning, has there been any teaching?"

These changes were accompanied by and reflected in the growth of interest in the accreditation of higher education programs and institutions. Not only were institutions desirous of gathering information about their success, a new and rapidly growing array of others outside the academy wanted similar information, especially with respect to the performance of the faculty and with respect to student learning as indicators of institutional success. That information was to be used as the basis for comparisons and for making decisions about the merit or worth of institutions and programs: clearly "evaluation" in Scriven's (1967) definition. Arreola (2006) discussed the effects of several paradigm shifts on current, higher education policy and practice, noting the dangers of ignoring the challenges they present. His conclusion was that higher education should be more aware of and responsive to the changes that surround it because those changes would be associated with policies that would be externally mandated if higher education did not initiate its own revisions and reforms. Demands for a national metric to compare colleges and universities and (in public institutions) to determine the extent of funding on the basis of students' performance on national tests bear out the prediction and the threat of inaction.

The press for accountability grew stronger over time, but for reasons noted above, the most available quantitative data about teaching and learning still came from the intensive investigation and use of student ratings of instruction in the late 1960s through the 1990s. There were over 2,000 publications and presentations on ratings topics during this time, and the percentages of institutions using ratings increased to over ninety percent (Seldin, 1999). The use of ratings data was partly a matter of convenience, but the result was that student ratings became overused, often—and unfortunately—as the only source of data about teaching effectiveness. There was a very predictable result: resistance, suspicion, and hostility toward student ratings, and the start of an early search for evidence that ratings were invalid and unreliable (Naftulin, Ware, and Donnelley, 1973; Rodin and Rodin, 1972). The early literature (Centra, 1979; Doyle, 1975) responded, and subsequent writing (Arreola, 1995; Berk, 2006; Braskamp, Brandenburg, and Ory, 1984; Centra, 1993; Cohen, 1981; Marsh, 1987; Theall and Franklin, 1990) consistently cautioned against the error of overreliance on a single source of information, but the cautions were largely ignored, and the search for evidence of invalidity continues to this day, with a focus on claims that ratings and evaluation in general have caused effects like grade inflation and the destruction of academic freedom (Haskell, 1997; Johnson, 2003).

This is the second unfortunate part of ratings history: the fact that such claims exist despite more than three decades of intensive investigation providing consistent evidence to the contrary (Aleamoni, 1987; Arreola, 2007; Centra, 1993; Cohen, 1980, 1981; Feldman, 1976, 1987, 1989, 1992a, 1992b, 1997; Marsh, 1987, 2007; Perry, Abrami, and Leventhal, 1979; Theall, Abrami, and Mets, 2001; Theall and Franklin, 1990). Many reasons have been offered for the ongoing and often contentious debate, and complaints about evaluation continue. Ebel's early comment (Ebel, 1983, p. 65), that "No corner of the university . . . lacks faculty who fulminate against student evaluations . . . ," still applies.

Why Does the Debate Remain So Difficult?

There are several reasons why the debate about evaluation and ratings continues, but the underlying problems in evaluation are more complex than a simple, valid-invalid or reliable-unreliable dichotomy suggests. The issues are often buried beneath bipolar rhetoric that has been supported, in one sense, by the negative influence of media sources that focus on ratings controversy rather than an accurate representation of research findings (Theall and Feldman, 2007). A more serious problem is pervasive poor practice in the development and use of ratings instruments, the analysis and reporting of data, and the interpretation and use of results. The field of evaluation has produced robust technical research supporting evaluation instrumentation and applications (for example, Feldman, 1989; Marsh, 2007), but has fallen short in its ability to integrate its findings into daily practice or to convince end users to accept and follow its advice. This problem was recognized two decades ago (Franklin and Theall, 1989; Theall and Franklin, 1990) and restated by Feldman (1998), who noted research on evaluation and student ratings was faced with ". . . a continuing quest and two unresolved issues."

One of those unresolved issues was the impact of situational variance that can affect local results in ways that seem to contradict reported mainstream research. Consider one of the most controversial issues in the student ratings area: the relationship of ratings and grades. Feldman's (1997) and Marsh's (2007) conclusions are that although the preponderance of research indicates an expected correlation of about .20 between ratings and student grades, it is entirely possible that in a particular set of circumstances, that figure could be considerably higher or lower. That, in itself, could cause much debate, but even in cases where local results match the meta-analytic average, there are consistently varying interpretations. Evaluation/ratings critics choose to interpret correlations like these as evidence of grade inflation that is caused by ratings. Proponents of evaluation/ratings claim that the results legitimize the research and ratings because a modest relationship is the expected outcome of good teaching leading to more effective learning, leading to more student satisfaction and thus, to higher ratings.

Even the choices of words used in stating such conclusions become part of the debate. Ratings instruments are most often surveys of opinions about students' experiences and observations. They are measures of teaching effectiveness in the sense that they have been developed to collect data about behaviors shown to relate to effective teaching. One can make a logical connection between reports of strong presentation skills, classroom management, classroom rapport, clarity, or the provision of information about course requirements, and effective teaching, but if the instruments ask students to report their satisfaction with a teacher or course, the relationship to effectiveness becomes less clear and begins to reflect something different. In other words, poor practice in instrument design can promote claims that ratings are ". . . nothing but a popularity contest" and in no way related to learning.

Another issue is related to the fact that contextual factors often determine evaluation process and performance expectations for faculty. The emphasis on process or outcomes and on the weight placed on teaching, scholarship, and service can change as a function of institutional type, mission, and history, as well as on the basis of disciplinary differences and departmental focus. For example, Cashin (1990) identified consistent patterns of disciplinary differences in ratings that match those in major validation studies of all widely used ratings instruments. Indeed, department-by-department differences in emphasis and performance expectations can result in completely different approaches, process, and decisions. Ignoring such differences puts the entire evaluation process at risk and invalidates it not because ratings are invalid measures, but because the results are not validly used. One cannot impose an externally developed process or instruments and assume that they will be successful locally, nor can one presume that even within a single institution, evaluation of faculty in one department is comparable to evaluation of faculty in another department.

The relationship of evaluation/ratings to student achievement, and thus their validity as a measure of teaching effectiveness, is yet another contentious issue. In support of the relationship of ratings to teaching effectiveness, proponents cite Cohen's (1981) meta-analysis of multisection course studies (replicated and repeated in the following decade) in which students' performance (tests and grades) correlated .43 with overall teacher ratings. Given similar content at similar levels with similar assessments neither designed nor corrected by the teachers involved, teachers in sections with better average student performance received higher ratings. To some, this is primary evidence of the validity of ratings as a measure of teaching effectiveness. However, some proponents perhaps go too far in their claims, and also state that Cohen's and subsequent results show that ratings measure learning. This is a mistake, because ratings questionnaires do not directly measure learning. To do so would require that they address content issues, and few if any ratings questionnaires do that.

Progress in Evaluation and Ratings

By the late 1980s, research on student ratings of teaching had explored most of the reliability and validity issues that had arisen, and major reviews of the literature were produced (for example, Marsh, 1987). Marsh revisited the literature over the next two decades and his conclusions are essentially the same, namely, that ratings are: multidimensional; reliable and stable; primarily a function of the instructor who teaches a course rather than the course that is taught; relatively valid against a variety of indicators of effective teaching; relatively unaffected by a variety of variables hypothesized as potential biases; and seen to be useful by faculty as feedback about their teaching, by students for use in course selection, and by administrators for use in personnel decisions (Marsh, 2007, p. 319). Recent and comprehensive discussions of teaching and learning and faculty evaluation issues can be found in several chapters in Perry and Smart (2007). The consensus one can infer from these chapters is that faculty evaluation should consider both process and outcomes, but, importantly, that there is no "one way" to carry out valid and reliable evaluation. Another implication is that faculty evaluation is less effective in the absence of sound programs for professional development and enrichment. The field of evaluation made definitional gains with the publication of Scriven's (1991) *Evaluation Thesaurus*. Shortly after that, Scriven (1994) added a pragmatic view of evaluation with a discussion of "The Duties of the Teacher." During the same period, interest in assessment increased and methods of gathering assessment data became known (Angelo and Cross, 1993; Cross and Steadman, 1996), and usable consequential data became more available, supporting the paradigm shift from teaching to learning (Barr and Tagg, 1995). Teaching effectiveness began to be viewed in terms of learning outcomes as well as pedagogy and instructional behaviors.

At the millennium, interest in a task-analytic approach to faculty roles, work, and skills led to a reconceptualization of the professoriate as a "meta-profession" that has its foundation in disciplinary expertise, but requires professional-level skills in several additional areas (Arreola, Theall, and Aleamoni, 2003; Theall and Arreola, 2006). Research on the meta-profession model (for example, Theall, Arreola, and Mullinix, 2009) reached four conclusions with major implications for faculty evaluation and development. The first was that contextual and individual variables affected perceptions about the roles, work, and skills of the faculty. These variables included institutional issues such as Carnegie type, size, history, and mission; disciplinary differences; and individual job or position (faculty or administrator). Given this finding, a related conclusion was that policy and practice in faculty evaluation and development should be based on an understanding of local definitions, priorities, and realities, as well as grounded in established research and literature. Another clear finding was that there were differences in perceptions about faculty expertise and the needs for meta-professional skills. Ratings of the expertise of the faculty were significantly lower than ratings of the need for certain skills in certain roles both in the general data set as well as in the results from individual institutions. The important implications of this finding were that at the institutional level, exploration of meta-professional skills could help to identify key areas of emphasis and performance criteria in evaluation, as well as identify areas in which to focus resources for professional development. Finally, other research (Theall and Cox, 2008; Theall, Mullinix, and Arreola, 2009) determined that quantitative exploration (that is, looking for significant differences of opinion in ratings of skills and needs) could be effectively supplemented by adding a qualitative component in a program of ongoing dialogue about meta-professional issues. Having data was a starting point for opening and sustaining dialogue about the profession. To paraphrase more specifically, one might title the ongoing local conversation as one related to, "What it means to be a faculty member at this institution." Making that determination is the first, best step toward improving faculty evaluation and professional development.

Toward the Future: Questions to Be Asked and Issues to Be Resolved

There are several changes in higher education that have not been fully addressed in the evaluation literature. One important issue is the extent to which teaching and learning in nontraditional settings are well understood. Particularly in distance and on-line instruction, contextual factors, situational dynamics, and individual variables can have different effects than they do in face-to-face instruction. The interface provided by complex technologies adds a degree of difficulty to research on these topics. In effect, the conclusions from established research (for example, the dimensions of teaching identified by Feldman, 1989) may or may not apply. Add to this is the fact that in many cases, the instruments used to evaluate teaching in on-line courses are the same ones used to evaluate face-to-face teaching. How, for example, does an inquiry about classroom rapport apply to an on-line course? What of questions pertaining to presentation skills? What skills do teachers and students need to be successful in these circumstances? Such questions have not been completely answered, and evaluation is compromised as a result. Not only is this a problem methodologically, it is an even more serious threat to equitable and defensible practice, and it puts faculty and institutions at risk.

Changes in the student population must be addressed as well. Do today's students hold the same understandings and expectations as those whose opinions are reflected in data from the first decades of evaluation and student ratings research? Are their levels or preparation, motivation, attention, and dedication the same, and if not, what are the differences and how do they affect teaching and learning? Are the teaching strategies shown to be successful in the 1980s successful in 2009? Do teachers need new sets of skills to be able to respond to these new students and new conditions? Change has become a new constant and this suggests that education must be able to respond to change. The immediate responsibility for this adaptability will fall to the faculty; that is, they must be able to understand and work with new students, new technologies, and new contexts in order to teach effectively. But the faculty cannot be held solely responsible for adapting to change. Higher education institutions must provide the resources needed by students and teachers. This leads to a final note

NEW DIRECTIONS FOR TEACHING AND LEARNING • DOI: 10.1002/tl

about a different kind of change that is affecting the nature of the professoriate.

Another important issue in evaluation is the increasing use of part-time, adjunct, and non-tenure-track faculty. Evaluation of teaching as it has been carried out is predicated on assumptions about the faculty and about careers in the professoriate. Promotion and tenure considerations have driven the criteria used in evaluation of teaching, scholarship, and service, but when teachers are hired on temporary contracts without the traditional career progression opportunities, how should they be evaluated? Have hiring practices changed the nature and focus of evaluation? Have these factors and the limited professional development support provided to non-full-time, non-tenure-track faculty affected the quality of teaching and learning? These questions are not psychometric or pedagogical, and they have not been well addressed in the evaluation literature.

Ultimately, the evaluation of teaching is a human resources matter. Faculty are the primary human resources of higher education because they are most responsible for carrying out the mission of higher education: the creation, transmission, application, and integration of knowledge. Yet policy and practice in faculty evaluation and professional enrichment have not evolved in ways that reflect the underlying premise that the function of these processes should be to maximize opportunities for faculty success. That success will lead to effective teaching and learning, to success for students, and to true accountability for institutions and for higher education.

References

Aleamoni, L. M. "Typical Faculty Concerns About Student Evaluation of Teaching." In L. M. Aleamoni (ed.), *Techniques for Evaluating and Improving Instruction.* New Directions for Teaching and Learning, no. 31. San Francisco: Jossey-Bass, 1987.

Angelo, T. A., and Cross, K. P. *Classroom Assessment Techniques: A Handbook for College Teachers.* (2nd ed.) San Francisco: Jossey Bass, 1993.

Arreola, R. A. *Developing a Comprehensive Faculty Evaluation System.* Bolton, Mass.: Anker, 1995.

Arreola, R. A. "Monster at the Foot of the Bed: Surviving the Challenge of Marketplace Forces on Higher Education." In S. Chadwick-Blossey and D. R. Robertson (eds.), *To Improve the Academy,* Vol. 24. Bolton, Mass.: Anker, 2006, pp. 15–28.

Arreola, R. A. *Developing a Comprehensive Faculty Evaluation System.* (3rd ed.) Bolton, Mass.: Anker, 2007.

Arreola, R. A., Theall, M., and Aleamoni, L. M. "Beyond Scholarship: Recognizing the Multiple Roles of the Professoriate." Paper presented at the annual meeting of the American Educational Research Association, Chicago, April 22, 2003. [http://www.cedanet.com/meta].

Barr, R. B., and Tagg, J. "From Teaching to Learning—A New Paradigm for Undergraduate Education." *Change,* 1995, 27(6), 13–25.

Berk, R. A. *Thirteen Strategies to Measure College Teaching.* Sterling, Va.: Stylus, 2006.

Braskamp, L., Brandenburg, D. C., and Ory, J. C. *Evaluating Teaching Effectiveness: A Practical Guide.* Newbury Park, Calif.: Sage, 1984.

Cashin, W. E. "Students Do Rate Different Academic Fields Differently." In M. Theall and J. Franklin (eds.), *Student Ratings of Instruction: Issues for Improving Practice*. New Directions for Teaching and Learning, no. 43. San Francisco: Jossey-Bass, 1990.

Centra, J. A. *Determining Faculty Effectiveness: Assessing Teaching, Research, and Service for Personnel Decisions and Improvement*. San Francisco: Jossey-Bass, 1979.

Centra, J. A. *Reflective Faculty Evaluation: Enhancing Teaching and Determining Faculty Effectiveness*. San Francisco: Jossey-Bass, 1993.

Cohen, P. A. "Effectiveness of Student-Rating Feedback for Improving College Instruction: A Meta-Analysis." *Research in Higher Education*, 1980, *13*, 321–341.

Cohen, P. A. "Student Ratings of Instruction and Student Achievement: A Meta-Analysis of Multisection Validity Studies." *Review of Educational Research*, 1981, *51*, 281–309.

Cronbach, L. J. "Course Improvement Through Evaluation." *The Record*, 1963, *64*(8), 672–683.

Cross, K. P., and Steadman, M. H. *Classroom Research: Implementing the Scholarship of Teaching*. San Francisco: Jossey-Bass, 1996.

Doyle, K. O. *Student Evaluation of Instruction*. Lexington, Mass.: D.C. Heath, 1975.

Ebel, K. A. *The Aims of College Teaching*. San Francisco: Jossey-Bass, 1983.

Feldman, K. A. "The Superior College Teacher from the Student's View." *Research in Higher Education*, 1976, *5*, 243–288.

Feldman, K. A. "Research Productivity and Scholarly Accomplishment of College Teachers as Related to Their Instructional Effectiveness: A Review and Exploration." *Research in Higher Education*, 1987, *26*(3), 227–298.

Feldman, K. A. "The Association Between Student Ratings of Specific Instructional Dimensions and Student Achievement: Refining and Extending the Synthesis of Data from Multisection Validity Studies." *Research in Higher Education,*1989, *30*, 583–645.

Feldman, K. A. "College Students' Views of Male and Female College Teachers. Part 1: Evidence from the Social Laboratory and Experiments." *Research in Higher Education*, 1992a, *33*(3), 317–375.

Feldman, K. A. "College Students' Views of Male and Female College Teachers. Part 2: Evidence from Students' Evaluations of Their Classroom Teachers. *Research in Higher Education*, 1992b, *33*(4), 415–474.

Feldman, K. A. "Identifying Exemplary Teachers and Teaching: Evidence from Student Ratings." In R. P. Perry and J. C. Smart (eds.), *Effective Teaching in Higher Education: Research and Practice*. New York: Agathon Press, 1997.

Feldman, K. A. "Reflections on the Effective Study of College Teaching and Student Ratings: One Continuing Quest and Two Unresolved Issues." In J. C. Smart (ed.), *Higher Education: Handbook of Theory and Research*. New York: Agathon Press, 1998.

Franklin, J., and Theall, M. "Who Reads Ratings: Knowledge, Attitudes, and Practices of Users of Student Ratings of Instruction." Paper presented at the 70th annual meeting of the American Educational Research Association, San Francisco, March 31, 1989. (ED 306 241)

Haskell, R. E. "Academic Freedom, Tenure, and Student Evaluation of Faculty: Galloping Polls in the 21st Century." *Education Policy Analysis Archives*, 1997, *5*(6) [http://olam.ed.asu.edu/epaa/v5n6.html].

Johnson, V. *Grade Inflation: A Crisis in Higher Education*. New York: Springer Verlag, 2003.

Marsh, H. W. "Students' Evaluations of University Teaching: Research Findings, Methodological Issues, and Directions for Future Research." *International Journal of Educational Research*, 1987, *11*, 253–388.

Marsh, H. W. "Students' Evaluations of University Teaching: Dimensionality, Reliability, Validity, Potential Biases, and Usefulness." In R. P. Perry and J. C. Smart (eds.), *The Scholarship of Teaching and Learning in Higher Education: An Evidence-Based Perspective*. New York: Springer, 2007, pp. 319–383.

Naftulin, D. H., Ware, J. E., and Donnelly, F. A. "The Doctor Fox Lecture: A Paradigm of Educational Seduction." *Journal of Medical Education,* 1973, *48,* 630–635.

Perry, R. P., Abrami, P. C., and Leventhal, L. "Educational Seduction: The Effect of Instructor Expressiveness and Lecture Content on Student Ratings and Achievement." *Journal of Educational Psychology,* 1979, 71(1), 107–116.

Perry, R. P., and Smart, J. C. (eds.). *The Scholarship of Teaching and Learning in Higher Education: An Evidence-Based Perspective.* Dordrecht, The Netherlands: Springer, 2007.

Remmers, H. H., and Brandenburg, G. C. "Experimental Data on the Purdue Rating Scale for Instruction." *Educational Administration and Supervision,* 1927, *13,* 519–527.

Rodin, M., and Rodin, B. "Student Evaluations of Teachers." *Science,* 1972, *177,* 1164–1166.

Scriven, M. "Methodology of Evaluation." In R. Tyler, R. Gagne, and M. Scriven (eds.), *Perspectives of Curriculum Evaluation.* Chicago: Rand McNally, 1967.

Scriven, M. *Evaluation Thesaurus.* (4th ed.) Newbury Park, Calif.: Sage, 1991.

Scriven, M. "Duties of the Teacher." *Journal of Personnel Evaluation in Education,* 1994, *8,* 151–184.

Seldin, P. *Changing Practices in Faculty Evaluation.* San Francisco: Jossey-Bass, 1999.

Stake, R. E. "The Countenance of Educational Evaluation." *The Record,* 1968, *68(7),* 523–545.

Taylor, P. A., and Maguire, T. O. *Readings in Curriculum Evaluation.* Dubuque, Iowa: Wm. C. Brown, 1966.

Theall, M., Abrami, P. A., and Mets, L. (eds.). *The Student Ratings Debate. Are They Valid? How Can We Best Use Them?* New Directions for Institutional Research, no. 109. San Francisco: Jossey-Bass, 2001.

Theall, M., & Arreola, R. A. (2006). The meta-profession of teaching. *NEA Higher Education Advocate,* 22(5), 5–8. Available at: http://www.cedanet.com/meta.

Theall, M., Arreola, R. A., and Mullinix, B. M. "Qualitatively Excavating Below the Quantitative Surface: An Action-Oriented, Case-Based Application of The Meta-Professional Model." Paper presented at the 90th annual meeting of the American Educational Research Association, San Diego, April 15, 2009. [http://www.cedanet.com/meta].

Theall, M., and Cox, M. D. "Faculty Learning Communities as Leadership Vehicles for Exploring the 'Meta-Profession' of the Professoriate and Revitalizing Collegial Campus Dialogue." Presentation at the 28th annual Lilly Conference on College Teaching, Oxford, Ohio, November 22, 2008.

Theall, M., and Feldman, K. A., 2007, Commentary and update of Feldman's (1997) "Identifying exemplary teachers and teaching: Evidence from student ratings." in R. P. Perry and J. C. Smart, (eds.), *The Scholarship of Teaching and Learning in Higher Education: An Evidence-Based Approach.* New York: Springer, pp. 130–143.

Theall, M., and Franklin, J. L. (eds.). *Student Ratings of Instruction: Issues for Improving Practice.* New Directions for Teaching and Learning, no. 43. San Francisco: Jossey-Bass, 1990.

Theall, M., Mullinix, B., and Arreola, R. A. "Promoting Dialogue and Action on 'Meta-Professional' Skills, Roles and Responsibilities." In L. B. Nilson and J. E. Miller (eds.), *To Improve the Academy,* Vol 28. San Francisco: Jossey-Bass, 2009.

MICHAEL THEALL *is associate professor of teacher education at Youngstown State University, Youngstown, Ohio, and the 2009 president of the Professional and Organizational Development Network in Higher Education. He received his Ph.D. from Syracuse University with a focus on instructional design, development, and evaluation. His research interests are the professoriate, faculty evaluation, student ratings of teaching, faculty professional development, college teaching and learning, and motivational issues.*

10

Changes have occurred since the first edition of New Directions for Teaching and Learning *was published. This chapter focuses on areas that have changed and on those that will probably not change as we move into the future.*

Hopes and Directions for the Future

Catherine M. Wehlburg

Many significant changes have taken place in higher education since the first issue of *New Directions for Teaching and Learning* (*NDTL*) was published in 1980. Reading through the previous chapters of this volume has certainly been a very interesting reminder of how much has changed. The purpose of this final chapter in this issue is to consider the directions that higher education may be taking in the future. What opportunities will we face? What obstacles will we need to overcome? Where will we be in the next decade or two? Although it is difficult to predict accurately what will happen in the future, there are many hints and indicators of what we can expect to impact higher education in the years ahead and how *NDTL* will help to define, refine, and discuss these changes. So, as I pull out my crystal ball and look into the future, I am optimistic and hopeful.

Things That Probably Will Change

Accountability. Accountability, assessment, and accreditation issues will continue to play a larger role within institutions of higher education. Already we are seeing that regional and specialized accreditors are increasing their requirements (Ewell, 2002) and the complexity of their reporting systems. And, with the recent reauthorization of the Higher Education Act, additional requirements will be added. Some of these requirements may impact teaching and learning. One example of a possible change requires that institutions with distance learning must demonstrate that the student who is registered for a particular course is the same student who takes the exams (Department of Education, 2009). This has the potential to change

NEW DIRECTIONS FOR TEACHING AND LEARNING, no. 123, Fall 2010 © Wiley Periodicals, Inc.
View this article online at wileyonlinelibrary.com. • DOI: 10.1002/tl.413

the way a faculty member designs exams or projects within an on-line course structure. However, not all of this change will be dire. Assessment and accountability practices may impact course design in positive ways. Faculty may now be required to list course-level learning objectives and demonstrate how students meet those objectives. Faculty can then use this information to enhance their courses. Although this may have been happening all along, requiring explicit assessment information for accountability can have a positive impact on teaching decisions and may improve learning.

Evaluation of teaching is another area within this topic of accountability. Most courses are evaluated, but, as Theall points out, there is much work to be done in terms of how these data are used and the methods for collecting data.

Technology.   One area that will continue to see exponential change is that of technology. Some of these changes will be seen as constructive, practical, and necessary. *Google* and *Wikipedia* are now entrenched terms in our vocabulary. And, how many of our current students spend time in the library stacks anymore? For that matter, how many faculty walk over to the library to find an article? Technology has given us access to data in more ways than we can count. The other side of this coin, of course, is that too much information can be overwhelming. Much of the technological access is open; it is up to the reader to determine if it is worthwhile or valid. These critical thinking skills are crucial as technology continues to grow and change. Technology in the classroom is also growing at a tremendous pace. What will it look like in the next five or ten years? And, as Kuhlenschmidt and Kacer explain in this volume, issues about technology are more about how we use it than about the technology tool itself. Using these new teaching tools to increase and enhance learning will be an ongoing challenge.

Changes in Student Demographics.   Students are changing. Our current students have grown up "in a world that is fundamentally different from previous generations" (Coomes and DeBard, 2004, p. 89). With changing technology, economics, and access to information, what will the next generation of students be like? It is clear that they will bring with them knowledge and skills for multitasking and accessing information that may be different from what faculty expect. College students will also bring parents with them—perhaps not into the classroom (although that has certainly happened)—but figuratively, as today's students contact their families much more often than ever before.

Changing immigration patterns and an increase in minority populations will also make our future students the most diverse group ever to enter into higher education. This may also mean that a larger percentage of students entering college will be first-generation students or underprepared. These changes in overall student demography will certainly impact issues of teaching and learning.

Changes in Student Expectations. As student demographics change, their expectations of what a college experience should be like will also change. Our current generation of students, called the "Net Gen" by Oblinger and Oblinger (2005), may expect immediate responses to e-mailed questions (even those that are sent in the early morning hours). They will be comfortable with many different types of technology, but they may have difficulties in synthesizing information across sources. Because of their experiences, they may not be accustomed to individual problem solving and may be more comfortable with group work than any previous generation. Their beliefs about their own needs for learning will impact how faculty design and teach their courses.

Structure of Educational Institutions. The typical structure of a major existing within a single department focusing on a single discipline is already beginning to shift. More interdisciplinary courses and programs are emerging and students are seeking out these programs. Our traditional college organization is becoming a little more loose—students are not just double majoring, they are creating new majors that synthesize multiple disciplines. When these are done well, tremendous learning can happen—and the restructuring (or even d econstructing) of traditional departments may happen in the future. Tagg's chapter, in this volume, helps to focus on an institution whose primary goal is to produce learning rather than instruction.

Things That May Not Change

Teaching and Learning Styles. Although the demographics and expectations of students may change, the overall teaching and learning pedagogies will remain. Even with the increasing rates of access to distance learning and fully on-line programs, college students will still attend regular courses, listen to lectures, and participate in classroom activities. Although there will be modifications and additions to these types of activities, there will still be certain foundational teaching and learning principles that will need to be addressed. As *NDTL* has done in the past, it will continue to highlight best practices and explore modifications to methods for teaching to improve learning.

Need for a Variety of Teaching/Learning Activities. Though many faculty teach using the same methods that their teachers taught them to use, there will still be an ongoing need to explore multiple pedagogies and teaching activities. New technologies will aid in this area, certainly, but the concept of multiple methods for teaching and for measuring student learning will still be crucial. Service-learning and community-based learning, as Zlotkowski and Duffy outline in this volume, will continue to expand on college campuses as faculty see their effectiveness in colleagues' courses. Thus, there will be an ongoing need to explore the scholarship of teaching and learning, as Hutchings has stated in this volume.

Theories of How and Why Learning Occurs. Research on learning has been ongoing and will continue to explore the conditions under which we learn. There will certainly be an expansion and a better understanding of these aspects of learning and how they impact teaching, but the value of this theoretical research will remain. Smith, in this volume, outlines the changes that have occurred over the past thirty years regarding the social aspect of learning. Modifications will continue to occur, but the underlying impact of communal learning will remain and even increase. The methods that students use to motivate and regulate their learning, as Svinicki notes in this volume, are crucial to understanding the psychology behind learning better.

Data collected concerning theories of how and why students learn will grow and change, but the need for these theories to be shared will not. *New Directions for Teaching and Learning* will remain a venue for sharing how these results are used in higher education.

The challenges that face higher education are daunting. Many within higher education are no longer content to sit in some ivory tower. Indeed, society is demanding that higher education become more responsive to social and economic needs. Parents want to be assured that their child will get a job after college, and those job skills and requirements are changing by the day. Students may view themselves as consumers who are "buying" a degree rather than having the opportunity to learn. Government officials are mandating what should be taught and when. But even with these (and other threats), there is a great deal of hope for the future of higher education. *New Directions for Teaching and Learning* will continue to provide to its readers information that is current, relevant, and timely.

As I gaze into my crystal ball for one last look, I see an exciting, stimulating, and sometimes startling future. I'm glad that we are all in this together.

References

Coomes, M. D., and DeBard, R. *Serving the Millennial Generation.* New Directions for Student Services, no. 106, San Francisco: Jossey-Bass, 2004.

Department of Education. *Federal Register,* 2009, 74. [http://edocket.access.gpo.gov/2009/pdf/E9–18368.pdf]

Ewell, P. *Perpetual Movement: Assessment After Twenty Years.* Boulder, Colo.: National Center for Higher Education Management Systems. 2002. [http://www.teaglefoundation.org/learning/pdf/2002_ewell.pdf]

Oblinger, D., and Oblinger J., *Educating the Net Generation.* Boulder, Colo.: EDUCAUSE, 2005. [http://www.educause.edu/ir/library/pdf/pub7101.pdf]

CATHERINE M. WEHLBURG *is the assistant provost for Institutional Effectiveness at Texas Christian University. She has taught psychology and educational psychology courses for more than a decade, serving as department chair for some of that time and then branching into faculty development and assessment. Dr. Wehlburg has worked with both the Higher Learning Commission of the North Central Association and the Commission on Colleges with the Southern Association of Colleges and Schools as an outside evaluator.*

NEW DIRECTIONS FOR TEACHING AND LEARNING • DOI: 10.1002/tl

INDEX

For a complete list of back issues, please visit www.josseybass.com/go/ndtl

stimulation of the senses, increasing crime rates, and a generally hurried existence. Professors are hardly immune from these forces, and the results cascade onto students, communities, and ultimately, society in general. In contrast to the traditional Western forms of education, which address rational consensus whole eschewing the subjective, a holistic pedagogy suggests that engaging spirituality in one's classroom and profession is necessary for addressing concerns regarding human development and achievement. More specifically, scholars now espouse the value of holistic teaching—teaching that encompasses not only the mind but the soul as well. The contributors in this volume offer diverse vantage points from which to understand the impact of spirituality on well-being, its influence on classroom pedagogy and interpersonal relationships with students and colleagues, and its utility as a coping mechanism. The authors use auto-ethnography to capture the diversity of their perspectives and to display the power of the reflective voice.
ISBN: 978-04705-92632

TL119   **Designing Courses for Significant Learning: Voices of Experience**
L. Dee Fink, Arletta Knight Fink
Higher education today is being called on to deliver a new and more powerful kind of education, one that prepares students to be more engaged citizens, better equipped to solve complex problems at work and better prepared to lead meaningful lives individually. To respond to this call, teachers in colleges and universities need to learn how to design more powerful kinds of learning into their courses. In 2003, Dee Fink published a seminal book, *Creating Significant Learning Experiences*, that offered teachers two major tools for meeting this need: the Taxonomy of Significant Learning and the model of Integrated Course Design. Since that time, educators around the world have found Fink's ideas both visionary and inspiring. This issue of *New Directions for Teaching and Learning* contains multiple stories of how college-level teachers have used these ideas in a variety of teaching situations, with subject matter ranging from the sciences to the humanities. Their conclusion? The ideas in Fink's book truly make a difference. When used properly, they lead to major improvements in the level of student engagement and the quality of student learning!
ISBN: 978-04705-54807

TL118   **Internationalizing the Curriculum in Higher Education**
Carolin Kreber
Internationalization is a looming policy issue in higher education—yet precisely what it can add to the student learning experience and what it means with regard to teaching and learning are far too infrequently discussed or written about. This volume explores different meanings and rationales underlying the notion of internationalization in higher education. Although internationalization efforts in higher education have become increasingly driven by economic considerations, finance is not an appropriate foundation for all initiatives, particularly those at the level of curriculum, where academic, social/cultural, ethical, political and even environmental rationales feature more strongly. The chapter authors provide a rich conceptual basis from which to appreciate concrete efforts directed at internationalizing curricula, and they describe nine cases of internationalization initiatives at the curricular level. The volume further suggests that consideration of internationalization in higher education must look both within specific programs and across programs. It cannot be separated from fundamental questions about the purposes of higher education and the roles of teachers, students, administrators, and the institution as a whole in fulfilling those purposes.
ISBN: 978-04705-37350

TL117 **Improving the Climate for Undergraduate Teaching and Learning in STEM Fields**
Roger G. Baldwin
The quality of undergraduate education in science, technology, engineering, and mathematics (STEM) fields has been a national concern since the time of Sputnik. In spite of many reports on the state of STEM undergraduate education and multiple reform efforts, time-worn patterns of instruction persist in many STEM classrooms and laboratories. It is increasingly clear that major improvements to STEM under-graduate education require the interest and active engagement of key stakeholders, including STEM instructors, academic administrators, disciplinary societies, and government policy-makers. This volume looks at the challenges of enhancing STEM education from the perspective of these different stakeholders. Each chapter provides an illumi-nating analysis of problems facing STEM education and suggests actions needed to strengthen STEM undergraduate education in a time when science and technology competence are more important than ever. The strategies advanced in this volume should be key elements of the coordinated, systemic effort necessary to implement lasting reform of STEM undergraduate education.
ISBN: 978-04704-97289

TL116 **Team-Based Learning: Small-Group Learning's Next Big Step**
Larry K. Michaelsen, Michael Sweet, Dean X. Parmelee
Team-Based Learning (TBL) is a unique form of small-group learning designed in and for the college classroom. TBL's special combination of incentives and corrective feedback quickly transforms groups into high-performance learning teams, with no time taken from the coverage of course content. In this issue of *New Directions for Teaching and Learning*, the authors describe the practical elements of TBL, how it can look in the classroom, and what they have learned as it has grown into an inter-disciplinary and international practice. Importantly, TBL is not about teaching but about learning. Several articles in this volume illustrate this emphasis by using TBL students' own words to reinforce key ideas.
ISBN: 978-04704-62126

TL115 **The Role of the Classroom in College Student Persistence**
John M. Braxton
This issue of *New Directions for Teaching and Learning* brings into sharp focus the complex role college and university faculty play in shaping the persistence and departure decisions of undergraduate students. The authors review practices ranging from curricular structures and instructional staffing policies to faculty teaching methods, and they offer recommendations for many common problems. Taken together, the chapters outline the elements of a scholarship of practice centered on keeping students in school. College and university presidents, chief academic affairs officers, academic deans, directors and staff members of campus-based centers for teaching, and individuals responsible for enrollment management will find a great deal of practical wisdom in this volume.
ISBN: 978-04704-22168

TL114 **Information Literacy: One Key to Education**
Margit Misangyi Watts
This issue draws on the expertise of librarians and faculty to highlight the central role of information literacy in higher education. The authors show how approaches to information literacy can be used to engage undergrad-uates in research and creative scholarship. The articles clarify definitions of information literacy and illustrate various means of curricular integration. Students regularly miss the relationship between the information-seeking process and the actual creation of knowledge. The authors in this issue

support infusing the undergraduate curriculum with research-based learning to facilitate students' ability to define research for themselves. Most importantly, this volume argues, students' information literacy leads beyond finding information—it actually involves their creating knowledge. Education should focus on inquiry, research, and discovery as a frame of mind. Our goal as educators should be to maintain and strengthen the *context* of learning while enhancing the *content* of a liberal education. This finally rests—as it always has—on a foundation of incorporating information literacy skills. Recent dramatic changes in the meaning of "information literacy" have left many educators scrambling to keep up. What has not changed is the importance of teaching students to find information that matters and then helping them figure out *why* it matters. These chapters can help us all integrate the new world of digital information into a relevant, timely approach to content and teaching practice.
ISBN: 978-04703-98715

TL113   **Educating Integrated Professionals: Theory and Practice on Preparation for the Professoriate**
Carol L. Colbeck, KerryAnn O'Meara, Ann E. Austin
This volume explores how to enhance doctoral education by preparing future faculty to integrate their work in two interrelated ways. The first mode encourages doctoral students—and their faculty mentors—to take advantage of the synergies among their teaching, research, and community service roles. The second mode of integration emphasizes connections between professional and academic aspects of faculty work. The authors draw on theories of identity development, professionalization, apprenticeship, socialization, mentoring, social networks, situated curriculum, concurrent curricula, and academic planning to illuminate some of the drawbacks of current education for the professoriate. They also point toward current programs and new possibilities for educating doctoral students who will be ready to begin their faculty careers as professionals who integrate teaching, research, and service.
ISBN: 978-04702-95403

TL112   **Curriculum Development in Higher Education: Faculty-Driven Processes and Practices**
Peter Wolf, Julia Christensen Hughes
Faculty within institutions of higher education are increasingly being asked to play leadership roles in curriculum assessment and reform initiatives. This change is being driven by quality concerns; burgeoning disciplinary knowledge; interest in a broader array of learning outcomes, including skills and values; and growing support for constructivist pedagogies and learning-centered, interdisciplinary curricula. It is essential that faculty be well prepared to take a scholarly approach to this work. To that end, this issue of *New Directions for Teaching and Learning* presents the frameworks used and lessons learned by faculty, administrators, and educational developers in a variety of curriculum assessment and development processes. Collectively, the authors in this volume present the context and catalysts of higher education curriculum reform, advocate for the Scholarship of Curriculum Practice (SoCP), provide examples of curricular assessment and development initiatives at a variety of institutional levels, suggest that educational developers can provide much support to such processes, and argue that this work has profound implications for the faculty role. Anyone involved in curriculum assessment and development will find food for thought in each chapter.
ISBN: 978-04702-78512

National Research Council book *How People Learn*. The chapters present case studies of working together to develop learning environments centered on challenge-based instruction. While the strategies and research come from engineering, they are applicable across disciplines to help students think about the process of problem solving.
ISBN: 07879-9574-6

TL107   **Exploring Research-Based Teaching**
Carolin Kreber
Investigates the wide scope research-based teaching, while focusing on two distinct forms. The first sees research-based teaching as student-focused, inquiry-based learning; students become generators of knowledge. The second perspective fixes the lens on teachers; the teaching is characterized by discipline-specific inquiry into the teaching process itself. Both methods have positive effects on student learning, and this volume explores research and case studies.
ISBN: 07879-9077-9

TL106   **Supplemental Instruction: New Visions for Empowering Student Learning**
Marion E. Stone, Glen Jacobs
Supplemental Instruction (SI) is an academic support model introduced over thirty years ago to help students be successful in difficult courses. SI teaches students how to learn via regularly scheduled, out-of-class collaborative sessions with other students. This volume both introduces the tenets of SI to beginners and brings those familiar up to speed with today's methods and the future directions. Includes case studies, how-to's, benefits to students and faculty, and more.
ISBN: 0-7879-8680-1

TL105   **A Laboratory for Public Scholarship and Democracy**
Rosa A. Eberly, Jeremy Cohen
Public scholarship has grown out of the scholarship-and-service model, but its end is democracy rather than volunteerism. The academy has intellectual and creative resources that can help build involved, democratic communities through public scholarship. Chapters present concepts, processes, and case studies from Penn State's experience with public scholarship.
ISBN: 0-7879-8530-9

TL104   **Spirituality in Higher Education**
Sherry L. Hoppe, Bruce W. Speck
With chapters by faculty and administrators, this book investigates the role of spirituality in educating the whole student while recognizing that how spirituality is viewed, taught, and experienced is intensely personal. The goal is not to prescribe a method for integrating spirituality but to offer options and perspectives. Readers will be reminded that the quest for truth and meaning, not the destination, is what is vitally important.
ISBN: 0-7879-8363-2

TL103   **Identity, Learning, and the Liberal Arts**
Ned Scott Laff
Argues that we must foster conversations between liberal studies and student development theory, because the skills inherent in liberal learning are the same skills used for personal development. Students need to experience core learning that truly influences their critical thinking skills, character development, and ethics. Educators need to design student learning encounters that develop these areas. This volume gives examples of how liberal arts education can be a healthy foundation for life skills.
ISBN: 0-7879-8333-0

TL96   **Online Student Ratings of Instruction**
Trav D. Johnson, D. Lynn Sorenson
Many institutions are adopting Web-based student ratings of instruction, or
are considering doing it, because online systems have the potential to save
time and money among other benefits. But they also present a number of
challenges. The authors of this volume have firsthand experience with
electronic ratings of instruction. They identify the advantages, consider costs
and benefits, explain their solutions, and provide recommendations on how
to facilitate online ratings.
ISBN: 0-7879-7262-2

TL95   **Problem-Based Learning in the Information Age**
Dave S. Knowlton, David C. Sharp
Provides information about theories and practices associated with problem-
based learning, a pedagogy that allows students to become more engaged in
their own education by actively interpreting information. Today's professors
are adopting problem-based learning across all disciplines to faciliate a
broader, modern definition of what it means to learn. Authors provide
practical experience about designing useful problems, creating conducive
learning environments, facilitating students' activities, and assessing
students' efforts at problem solving.
ISBN: 0-7879-7172-3

TL94   **Technology: Taking the Distance out of Learning**
Margit Misangyi Watts
This volume addresses the possibilities and challenges of computer
technology in higher education. The contributors examine the pressures to
use technology, the reasons not to, the benefits of it, the feeling of being a
learner as well as a teacher, the role of distance education, and the place of
computers in the modern world. Rather than discussing only specific
successes or failures, this issue addresses computers as a new cultural
symbol and begins meaningful conversations about technology in general
and how it affects education in particular.
ISBN: 0-7879-6989-3

TL93   **Valuing and Supporting Undergraduate Research**
Joyce Kinkead
The authors gathered in this volume share a deep belief in the value of
undergraduate research. Research helps students develop skills in problem
solving, critical thinking, and communication, and undergraduate
researchers' work can contribute to an institution's quest to further
knowledge and help meet societal challenges. Chapters provide an overview
of undergraduate research, explore programs at different types of
institutions, and offer suggestions on how faculty members can find ways to
work with undergraduate researchers.
ISBN: 0-7879-6907-9

TL92   **The Importance of Physical Space in Creating Supportive Learning
Environments**
Nancy Van Note Chism, Deborah J. Bickford
The lack of extensive dialogue on the importance of learning spaces in
higher education environments prompted the essays in this volume. Chapter
authors look at the topic of learning spaces from a variety of perspectives,
elaborating on the relationship between physical space and learning, arguing
for an expanded notion of the concept of learning spaces and furnishings,
talking about the context within which decision making for learning spaces

takes place, and discussing promising approaches to the renovation of old learning spaces and the construction of new ones.
ISBN: 0-7879-6344-5

TL91   **Assessment Strategies for the On-Line Class: From Theory to Practice**
Rebecca S. Anderson, John F. Bauer, Bruce W. Speck
Addresses the kinds of questions that instructors need to ask themselves as they begin to move at least part of their students' work to an on-line format. Presents an initial overview of the need for evaluating students' on-line work with the same care that instructors give to the work in hard-copy format. Helps guide instructors who are considering using on-line learning in conjunction with their regular classes, as well as those interested in going totally on-line.
ISBN: 0-7879-6343-7

TL90   **Scholarship in the Postmodern Era: New Venues, New Values, New Visions**
Kenneth J. Zahorski
A little over a decade ago, Ernest Boyer's *Scholarship Reconsidered* burst upon the academic scene, igniting a robust national conversation that maintains its vitality to this day. This volume aims at advancing that important conversation. Its first section focuses on the new settings and circumstances in which the act of scholarship is being played out; its second identifies and explores the fresh set of values currently informing today's scholarly practices; and its third looks to the future of scholarship, identifying trends, causative factors, and potentialities that promise to shape scholars and their scholarship in the new millennium.
ISBN: 0-7879-6293-7

TL89   **Applying the Science of Learning to University Teaching and Beyond**
Diane F. Halpern, Milton D. Hakel
Seeks to build on empirically validated learning activities to enhance what and how much is learned and how well and how long it is remembered. Demonstrates that the movement for a real science of learning—the application of scientific principles to the study of learning—has taken hold both under the controlled conditions of the laboratory and in the messy real-world settings where most of us go about the business of teaching and learning.
ISBN: 0-7879-5791-7

TL88   **Fresh Approaches to the Evaluation of Teaching**
Christopher Knapper, Patricia Cranton
Describes a number of alternative approaches, including interpretive and critical evaluation, use of teaching portfolios and teaching awards, performance indicators and learning outcomes, technology-mediated evaluation systems, and the role of teacher accreditation and teaching scholarship in instructional evaluation.
ISBN: 0-7879-5789-5

TL87   **Techniques and Strategies for Interpreting Student Evaluations**
Karron G. Lewis
Focuses on all phases of the student rating process—from data-gathering methods to presentation of results. Topics include methods of encouraging meaningful evaluations, mid-semester feedback, uses of quality teams and focus groups, and creating questions that target individual faculty needs and interest.
ISBN: 0-7879-5789-5